LUKE

WESLEY BIBLE STUDIES

wphonline.com

CONTENTS

INTRODUCTION

Notes from the Doctor

Doctors write notes for their patients (prescriptions) and about each patient visit—the nature of any ailments, a summary of the examination, any treatment given, and follow-up recommendations. Referrals to other doctors also involve written correspondence.

Luke, the person God used to write the inspired gospel that bears his name, was a doctor. We might say his gospel is an authoritative, accurate collection of his notes. But Dr. Luke's notes were not about a patient; they were all about another doctor, Jesus, the Great Physician. Luke's primary audience was the Greeks, who believed their culture could produce wise, perfect individuals. Undoubtedly, Luke wanted them to understand that Jesus was all-wise and perfect. But first and foremost, Luke wrote to present Jesus as the perfect Son of Man, who came to save us (see Luke 19:10).

BIRTH RECORDS

Luke wrote first about two miraculous births. The first involved a very old couple, Zechariah and Elizabeth. Zechariah was a Jewish priest, and Elizabeth was barren. Both were godly members of a remnant that was looking for the arrival of Israel's messiah. God granted them a baby boy, John, who heralded the Messiah's imminent coming.

The second miraculous birth was that of our Savior. He was born of Mary, a godly virgin who considered herself the Lord's servant (Luke 1:38). Jesus' birth was an occasion of great rejoicing, and it was good news for all people.

DIAGNOSIS OF SIN

Luke wrote that John the Baptist fearlessly and faithfully summoned the nation to repent and be baptized in preparation for the Messiah's arrival. John exposed hypocrisy and denounced self-righteousness.

Luke's notes cite many cases of sin, including the most heinous sin of all: the crucifixion of our Lord and Savior. He clearly detailed events leading up to the crucifixion: betrayal by Judas, Jesus' arrest, Peter's denial of Him, the beatings He endured, arraignment before the political authorities, and Pilate's cowardly act of heeding the crowd's demand that Jesus be crucified.

THE GREAT PHYSICIAN'S POWER TO
HEAL AND FORGIVE

Luke's gospel also overflows with accounts of the healing and forgiveness Jesus brought to needy individuals. No one lay beyond His power and love. Tax collectors, a woman of bad reputation, a centurion's servant, and a hemorrhaging woman who had been treated unsuccessfully by a number of doctors were among the many He healed and forgave.

THE GREAT PHYSICIAN WILL SEE YOU NOW

As you progress through this study, may your love and devotion for Jesus increase! While you marvel at His sinless character and selfless ministry, recognize that the Great Physician is always available to hear your concerns and meet your needs. His office is never closed!

WHO, ME?

Luke 1:5–7, 11–20, 26–38

God works in our lives through answered prayers
and unexpected blessings.

Waiting is often hard to do. For example, when you were a child, didn't you find it hard to wait for Christmas? When you rode in your parents' car toward a distant location, how often did you ask, "Are we there yet?" When you were a student, was it hard to wait for summer break? Now that you are an adult, you may find it hard to wait for a promotion, raise, vacation, or even medical test results.

This study features a few righteous Jews who were waiting patiently for the arrival of the Messiah. Their patience and the way God rewarded that patience encourage us to wait patiently on God.

COMMENTARY

The gospel of Luke, inspired by God to possibly the only Gentile writer of the New Testament, is a unique account of the life of Jesus for which all of Christendom is indebted and grateful. There are details of Jesus' life recorded by no other gospel writer that comprise about 60 percent of the whole book. Only the gospel of John is more unique with over 90 percent of its material unlike any of the other three gospels.

The prologue of Luke is a literary gem, written in the best Greek style of the whole New Testament, second only to the book of Hebrews. We have reason to believe that Luke lived at Antioch, Syria, and may have studied medicine at the University of Tarsus, where there was a famous medical school in the first century of the Christian era. Since Tarsus was the hometown of Saul, who became the apostle Paul, it is possible that Luke and Paul may have been students at the same time at the university. Both men, well-trained and scholarly, later ministered together through western Asia Minor and southern Europe.

A notably accurate historian, Dr. Luke was a general practitioner. He would have been challenged to tackle the project of making a thorough investigation of Jesus' life for Theophilus, a man of considerable distinction. Theophilus ("Lover of God" or "Loved by God") even may have paid for the publication of both the gospel of Luke and the book of Acts, also believed to have been written by Luke. Some authorities think Luke and Acts may have been circulated together after both had been composed (Luke 1:1–4; Acts 1:1–2). We learn by tradition that Luke never married and lived to age eighty-four, thus being free to spend whatever time was necessary to write carefully and accurately both accounts of Jesus' life and much of the apostle Paul's life.

Because of its various emphases, the gospel of Luke has been called the gospel of prayer (there are twenty references to Jesus praying or His teaching on prayer), the gospel of Eucharistic hymns (five hymns are found in chapters 1 and 2), the gospel of salvation by grace (ten times the word for *evangelize* is used and there are eight uses of the word *grace*), the gospel of the poor, the gospel of humility, the gospel of the Holy Spirit, and the gospel of the universality of God's provisions for the human family.

Luke's gospel is the longest of all four gospels and, with the book of Acts, his contribution to the New Testament is more substantive than any of the other seven known writers of the New Testament. Luke presented Jesus as the Son of Man instead of the Son of God, as did John in his gospel. The great interpolation of Luke is found in chapters 10–18, where the ministry of Jesus is primarily in Perea. Only Luke recorded as much of the ministry of Jesus there. Of a total of thirty-six miracles in the four gospels, Luke recorded twenty. Of the thirty parables in the four gospels, Luke recorded nineteen. All students of the New Testament will be blessed by what the Holy Spirit led Luke to write.

Zechariah and Elizabeth Had No Children (Luke 1:5–7)

Herod (v. 5) the Great (both because of his construction projects — aqueducts, Masada, and the temple in Jerusalem — and his terrible wickedness) is mentioned here to date the time when John the Baptist was to be born, six months before Jesus (probably 5 or 6 B.C.). Because of his cruelty in ordering the slaughter of babies in and around Bethlehem after Jesus was born, Herod was greatly feared. The parents of John the Baptist were **Zechariah** and **Elizabeth**, who were **descendant** from the **priestly** line **of Aaron. Both of them were upright . . . observing all the Lord's commandments and regulations blamelessly. But they had no children . . . and they were both well along in years** (vv. 5–7).

WORDS FROM WESLEY

Luke 1:6

Walking in all the moral *commandments, and* ceremonial *ordinances, blameless* — How admirable a character! May our behaviour be thus unblameable, and our obedience thus sincere and universal! (ENNT)

As a Jewish priest, Zechariah worked at the temple teaching the Scriptures, directing the worship services, and tending to the temple's upkeep. It is estimated that there were twenty thousand priests at this time, divided into twenty-four separate groups of nearly a thousand each, who took their turn in serving. Early in the morning, a priest on duty would enter the Holy Place and burn incense. It was at such a time that the Lord gave a special message to the elderly couple. They were going to have a baby, chosen because they **were upright in the sight of God** (v. 6).

Gabriel Startled Zechariah (Luke 1:11–20)

Angels are spirit beings created by God to do His will. Only two are mentioned by name in the Bible—Michael (Dan. 10:13, 21; 12:1; Jude 9; Rev. 12:7) and Gabriel (Dan. 8:16; 9:21; Luke 1:19, 26). In this text, Gabriel is called the **angel of the Lord** (v. 11). He was **standing at the right side of the altar of incense**, and because of his sudden and unexpected appearance, **when Zechariah saw him, he was startled and was gripped with fear** (vv. 11–12). Throughout the Bible, awe, surprise, fear, and consternation are almost universal reactions to angelic encounters.

WORDS FROM WESLEY
Luke 1:12

Zacharias was troubled—Although he was accustomed to converse with God, yet we see he was thrown into a great consternation, at the appearance of his angelical messenger, nature not being able to sustain the sight. Is it not then an instance of the goodness as well as of the wisdom of God, that the services, which these heavenly spirits render us, are generally invisible? (ENNT)

The message of Gabriel was both comforting and exciting: **"Elizabeth will bear you a son** because **your prayer has been heard"** (v. 13). Furthermore, **"He will be a joy and delight to you, and many will rejoice . . . for he will be great in the sight of the Lord"** (vv. 14–15). The joy this child would bring was not only because his parents had prayed for him, but also because he was to be great as the forerunner of the Messiah. Several directions were given to Elizabeth and Zechariah. His **name** was to be **John** (meaning "the Lord is gracious"). He was **never to take wine or other fermented drink, and he will be filled with the Holy Spirit even from birth** (vv. 13, 15).

The qualification of John to be the forerunner of Jesus was not only because of the seal of the Holy Spirit, but also because he was to be preserved in purity as part of the law of a Nazirite. This ancient vow, instituted in Numbers 6:1–8, was one that Samson, and possibly Samuel, took in holy consecration to God's service. John would **go on before the Lord, in the spirit and power of Elijah**, turning **many of the people of Israel . . . back to the Lord . . . to make ready a people prepared for the Lord** (Luke 1:16–17).

Zechariah questioned that this could happen and said, **"I am an old man and my wife is well along in years"** (v. 18). Since Zechariah doubted, **Gabriel** responded: **"I stand in the presence of God, and I have been sent to speak to you and to tell you this good news. . . . You will be silent and not able to speak until the day this happens"** (vv. 19–20). We all must learn that what God has promised He will accomplish at the right time.

Gabriel Troubled Mary (Luke 1:26–38)

Six months after Zechariah had been told his wife was to have a baby, **God sent the angel Gabriel to Nazareth, a town in Galilee, to a virgin** named **Mary** (vv. 26–27). This is only the fourth time in the Bible that Gabriel is named. His name means "God is mighty," and each time he visited, he made an announcement or gave direction or information to Daniel (Dan. 8:16; 9:21), Zechariah (Luke 1:19), or **Mary** (v. 26). The words of Gabriel to Mary were, **"Greetings, you who are highly favored! The Lord is with you. . . . Do not be afraid, Mary, you have found favor with God"** (vv. 28, 30).

WORDS FROM WESLEY
Luke 1:28

Hail, thou highly favoured; the Lord is with thee; blessed art thou among women—Hail is the salutation used by our Lord, to the women after His resurrection: *Thou art highly favoured*, or *hast found favour with God*, ver. 30 is no more than was said of Noah, Moses, and David. *The Lord is with thee*, was said to Gideon (Judg. 6:12), *and blessed shall she be above women*, of Jael (Judg. 5:24). This salutation gives no room for any pretence of paying adoration to the Virgin: as having no appearance of a prayer, or of worship offered to her. (ENNT)

Mary was greatly troubled at Gabriel's **words and wondered what** the **greeting** meant (v. 29). The angel's words were, **"You will be with child and give birth to a son, and you are to give him the name Jesus"** (v. 31). Although every young woman among the Jews knew the prophecy of a coming messiah and wondered who might be chosen to be His mother, Mary was utterly amazed and probably with furrowed brow asked, **"How will this be . . . since I am a virgin?"** (v. 34). Mary was a poor, young, pure woman, who was **pledged to be married to a man named Joseph, a descendant of David** (v. 27). The pledge in Jewish custom was more than our contemporary idea of engagement. A pledge was legally binding and could be broken only by a legal divorce. Thus, Joseph would have needed to divorce Mary quietly, as he had considered, if the pledge was severed, according to Matthew (Matt. 1:18–19).

The Lord's blessing on Mary to be the mother of the Messiah brought her much pain. She found it necessary to stay with Elizabeth, probably to escape the scorn and near divorce by Joseph. Her son, Jesus, was going to be viciously attacked and murdered. But **He** was to **be great and . . . the Lord God will give him the throne of his father David, and he will reign over the**

house of Jacob forever; his kingdom will never end (Luke
1:32–33). Many centuries before, God had promised that David's
kingdom would last forever (2 Sam. 7:16). This promise was fulfilled in Christ, who was a direct descendent of David. Thus,
Jesus our Lord will rule and reign throughout eternity.

WORDS FROM WESLEY

Luke 1:37

The omnipresent God sees and knows all the properties of the
beings that He hath made. He knows all the connexions, dependen-
cies, and relations, and all the ways wherein one of them can affect
another. In particular, He sees all the inanimate parts of the creation,
whether in heaven above, or in the earth beneath. He knows how the
stars, comets, or planets above influence the inhabitants of the earth
beneath; what influence the lower heavens, with their magazines of
fire, hail, snow, and vapours, winds, and storms, have on our planet;
and what effects may be produced in the bowels of the earth by fire,
air, or water; what exhalations may be raised therefrom, and what
changes wrought thereby; what effects every mineral or vegetable
may have upon the children of men: All these lie naked and open to
the eye of the Creator and Preserver of the universe. . . .

And is the Creator and Preserver of the world unconcerned for
what He sees therein? . . . Does He sit at ease in the heaven, without
regarding the poor inhabitants of earth? It cannot be. He hath made
us, not we ourselves, and He cannot despise the work of His own
hands. We are His children: And can a mother forget the children of
her womb? Yea, she may forget; yet will not God forget us! On the
contrary, He hath expressly declared, that as His "eyes are over all
the earth," so He "is loving to every man, and his mercy is over all
his works." Consequently, He is concerned every moment for what
befalls every creature upon earth; and more especially for everything
that befalls any of the children of men. (WJW, vol. 6, 316–317)

Gabriel told Mary, when she asked how she could be the
mother of Jesus, **"The Holy Spirit will come upon you, and
the power of the Most High will overshadow you. So the holy
one to be born will be called the Son of God"** (Luke 1:35).

The name Jesus was a familiar name among the Jews. It means "the Lord saves" and is the Greek form of the Hebrew Joshua, the most well-known being the Joshua who led the children of Israel into the Promised Land (Josh. 1:1–2). Jesus came to lead those who receive Him into everlasting life. This symbolism was striking to the Jews of Jesus' day, setting Him apart as a special person, the incarnate Son of God.

Mary was informed that **even Elizabeth**, her cousin, was **going to have a child in her old age, and she who was said to be barren** was **in her sixth month. For nothing is impossible with God** (Luke 1:36–37). **The angel left** Mary when she answered, **"I am the Lord's servant. . . . May it be to me as you have said"** (v. 38). It is possible that at the moment of Mary's faith and in her submission to the Lord's will the miraculous conception (not immaculate conception, the term that describes the belief that Mary was born without sin) took place. It was John Wesley who observed that the greatest proof that God saves us and sanctifies us in a moment is because any work in a believer's life must, of necessity, come by faith. In that moment of belief, the work of grace occurs.

DISCUSSION

Generally, we regard medical doctors as reputable men and women of science who are concerned about our well-being. Dr. Luke, a reputable man of science in the first century, wrote his gospel with concern for our faith and our overall spiritual health.

1. Read Luke 1:1–3. How does this passage confirm and/or strengthen your belief in Jesus as a real, historic person?

2. How would you describe the character of Zechariah and his wife?

3. Why do you agree or disagree that Zechariah and Elizabeth were part of a spiritual remnant in Israel?

4. How does Luke 5:11–20 encourage you to pray?

5. How do you believe John's birth would cause many people to rejoice?

6. How does Zechariah's renewed hearing encourage you to trust God to keep His word?

7. What characteristics in Mary's life would you like to incorporate into yours?

8. Read Luke 1:38. How can you truthfully and confidently say that you are the Lord's servant?

PRAYER

Father, we see in the willing service of these faithful followers a challenge to live a life set apart for Your use. Purify us from anything that would soil us or keep us from being useful in Your service.

2

GOOD NEWS FOR ALL

Luke 2:1–20

Good news is for all people.

Abraham Lincoln quipped that God must have loved the common people, because He made so many of them. Honest Abe may have been right, although God certainly loves "uncommon" people too. God didn't announce the birth of His Son Jesus first to the cultural elite but to shepherds, whose station in life was distant from the rich and powerful. They heard that Jesus' birth was good news for all people and, after visiting God's Lamb, they spread the word about Him.

Like the shepherds, we have received the good news, and we are called to share it.

COMMENTARY

Jesus' birth is perhaps the most famous birth in history, and rightly so. The universal nature of Christ's advent is summarized in the message of the angels found in Luke 2:10: "good news of great joy that will be for all the people."

Jesus' coming and His death and resurrection are not just for Jewish people, but for "all the people." Jesus died for the sins of the world, not just those of a single nation or race.

A Census Was Taken (Luke 2:1–3)

Luke's mention of **Caesar Augustus** (v. 1) and other political leaders gives chronological context to the book, helping to establish dates. The **decree** was simply a ruling passed on by Caesar. It was to be followed without delay. **A census** was taken about every fourteen years. **Quirinius** and his country, **Syria** (v. 2), are mentioned to help further pinpoint the authenticity of the book and the census. Luke was careful to use specific details whenever possible. **The entire Roman world** (v. 1) was literally the entire world, with the word **Roman** being added by translators for clarity. But the Greek word *oikoumeneen* sometimes refers specifically to the land of Israel, and history verifies that a census was taken in Israel with a larger census some years later. So perhaps a better understanding of where the census took place would be "the entire Jewish world."

It was the custom of the day that people **went to** their **own town to register** (v. 3) themselves, their occupations, and their families. The purpose for the census was probably taxation. For other nations under Roman rule, a census also served as a notice of those eligible for military service. But the Jewish people were exempt from Roman military obligations.

Jesus Was Born in Bethlehem (Luke 2:4–7)

The hand of God is seen in the calling for a census because it required **Joseph** (v. 4) to travel home to Bethlehem. It was God's will for Jesus to be born in Bethlehem as the prophets foretold in Micah 5:2 and as recorded in Matthew 2:6. **Nazareth** is about eighty miles from **Bethlehem**, which is known as the **town of David** (Luke 2:4) because King David grew up there. The prophets foretold the lineage of the Messiah through David in Jeremiah 33:15–17. All this detail validates Jesus' birthright as the Messiah.

Mary was **pledged to be married** (Luke 2:5) to Joseph and was expecting a child, Jesus. **Pledged** actually means she was betrothed, or in today's terms, engaged. Betrothal was a serious commitment, sometimes requiring a certificate of divorce to break.

It must have been a difficult trip for the two of them. Some historians tell us that Mary was not obligated to make the trip.

That being said, she may have gone because she realized her role in fulfilling the prophetic voice of the Old Testament. Verse 6 tells us the time of pregnancy was the ninth month, because **the baby** was **born** while they were in Bethlehem. Her **firstborn** (v. 7) is mentioned to reaffirm Mary's virginity. There were no older siblings and there was no sexual union between Joseph and Mary prior to Jesus' birth (see Matt. 1:25).

WORDS FROM WESLEY

Luke 2:6

And while they were there, the days were fulfilled that she should be delivered—Mary seems not to have known that the child must have been born in Bethlehem, agreeably to the prophecy. But the providence of God took care for it. (ENNT)

Cloths (Luke 2:7) were long linen strips that bundled the baby tightly. Hospitals wrap infants in a similar way today using blankets. There was **no room for them in the inn** (v. 7) because the small town was flooded with people registering for the census. Typical Jewish custom leads us to expect the young couple to stay with relatives. It may have been that their family's homes were already full to overflowing as was the inn. Sometimes the innkeeper is portrayed as a gruff and uncaring soul, but the biblical record doesn't offer such detail. The reason there was no room in the inn is because others arrived before Joseph and Mary and occupied all the rooms. Bethlehem was crowded, and there were more people than accommodations. The **manger** (v. 7) may have been a feeding trough. Some historians feel the actual location of Jesus' birth was either a cave-like place where shepherds kept their flocks in inclement weather or in the courtyard of the inn where travelers boarded their beasts of burden. Whichever, the symbolism is profound. The Lord of all creation came to earth and there was no room for Him. Similarly, many people today are too busy for Jesus—they have no room for Him in their lives.

WORDS FROM WESLEY

Luke 2:7

She laid him in the manger—Perhaps it might rather be translated *in the stall*. They were lodged in the ox-stall, fitted up on occasion of the great concourse, for poor guests. *There was no room for them in the inn*—Now also, there is seldom room for Christ in an inn. (ENNT)

Another interesting parallel in this story is the play on the term **Bethlehem** (v. 4), which means "house of bread." Jesus referred to himself as the "bread of life" in John 6:35. So, the house of bread produced that which feeds the whole world—Jesus, the Bread of Life.

It is fascinating that the Sovereign Lord of all creation became a helpless child. The Creator became one of the created. The all-powerful one became the vulnerable one. The one who used political giants and kings to control the behavior of many people and orchestrate a census became the infant child of a humble carpenter.

For Caesar, it was business as usual—take the census. For Joseph and Mary, it was the realization that they were part of the greatest spiritual and religious event in the history of the world at that time—the birth of Christ. For the angels, it was the greatest announcement the world had ever heard—a Savior had been born. For the shepherds, it was the highest honor they would ever have—to be the first to worship the Christ child. For us, it is the greatest opportunity we will ever have—to serve Jesus and proclaim Him through our testimony, teaching, and lifestyle.

Angels Proclaimed the Birth of Christ to Shepherds (Luke 2:8–20)

The **shepherds living out in the fields** (v. 8) were hardworking men who took their job seriously. They kept **watch over their flocks at night** (v. 8) instead of sleeping on the job. For the announcement about the birth of Jesus to come to ordinary, blue-collar workers is significant and symbolic. It is symbolic in that Jesus referred to himself as the Good Shepherd in John 10:11. It is significant in that shepherds were thought to be "unclean" people. They were considered such because their jobs often kept them away from temple worship for weeks at a time. They often neglected the rules of hand-washing and so forth that meant so much to the religious elite. The first people to hear about the birth of Jesus from the angels were a group of common men busy at work. Some historians feel that these shepherds were tending the flocks used for temple worship. If so, the symbolism of the angelic annunciation to them is even more incredible. The birth of Jesus, the Lamb of God who would take away the sins of the world, came to shepherds who may have tended the flocks of sacrificial lambs for temple sacrifice.

An angel . . . appeared (Luke 2:9) first and then was accompanied by many others in verse 13. It must have been quite a sight for those seasoned shepherds to see the brilliance of the angels against the darkness of the night. The **glory of the Lord** (v. 9) refers to this brilliance or brightness. Paul experienced something similar on the road to Damascus. It is also reminiscent of Moses' face, which shone with the glory of God and required a veil to cover it. Heaven has no luminaries such as the sun or moon. The radiance of the Lord is all that is needed. When the angels came to earth, they shone with the brilliance of heaven and it caused the shepherds to be afraid.

The angelic message was profound—**"Do not be afraid"** (v. 10). A supernatural appearance of this kind would frighten anyone. The shepherds were no exception. The angel's message was of **good news of great joy** (v. 10). What a wonderful message that still brings great joy today, the birth of Jesus. We all enjoy hearing good news. It cheers our hearts and souls to hear that our friends and loved ones are faring well. Even more so does the good news about Jesus bring cheer and joy to our hearts and souls. This message is **for all the people** (v. 10) not just for Jews or shepherds. The entire world is to hear the glorious truth about the Son of God born in Bethlehem. He is **a Savior** (v. 11) who saves us from the guilt and consequences of our sins. He is **Christ** or Messiah—the Anointed One who will redeem the world and set things right. The sign of truth given to this announcement is the baby's location: **wrapped in cloths and lying in a manger** (v. 12). The shepherds would have to look for the child, but they knew where mangers were located.

WORDS FROM WESLEY

Luke 2:14

Glory be to God in the highest; on earth peace; good-will towards men—The shouts of the multitude are generally broken into short sentences. This rejoicing acclamation strongly represents the piety and benevolence of these heavenly spirits: as if they had said, *Glory be to God in the highest heavens:* Let all the angelic legions resound His praises. For with the Redeemer's birth, *peace*, and all kind of happiness, come down to dwell *on earth:* Yea, the overflowings of divine *good will* and favour, are now exercised *towards men.* (ENNT)

A company of angels appeared and began praising God. Then they proclaimed a message: **"Glory to God in the highest"**

(v. 14). Only our highest praise is worthy of such a loving and self-giving Lord. **"On earth peace to men"** (v. 14)—one thing the world can agree on is the desire for global peace and the ability to get along with one another. In Jesus, this can be accomplished. Neither ideology nor philosophy nor philanthropy can bring about world harmony. It is only in Jesus that global peace can be found. Oh, that the world would unite in praises to the one who came as the Savior of the world!

"Let's go to Bethlehem" (v. 15) was the response of the shepherds. They could do nothing else. Their hearts compelled them to find the child announced by angels. They did find Him, and His parents too. The Bible says they **hurried off** (v. 16). Once we know the will of God, it behooves us to do it quickly. There is a time to wait and a time to get going. This was a time to hurry, and the shepherds knew it well. They were eager to see what God was doing in the world. Their response after finding the Christ child was to **spread the word** (v. 17) about Him. Once we find Jesus, we want to tell others about Him. He is the greatest thing to happen in our lives. We cannot contain the **good news of great joy** (v. 10) that comes to us when we find Jesus. Our lives are forever changed, transformed into the fragrance of holiness, a thing of beauty, a reflection of the Master.

All who heard it were amazed (v. 18) because the message was incredible and the men who told it were trustworthy and hard-working. The story they told was so wonderful it had to be true.

Mary treasured . . . these things and pondered them in her heart (v. 19) as any mother would do. Her heart overflowed with joy at the Lord's work in her marriage, her childbearing, and her son. The treasures of her heart were not temporary; she **pondered them**. Mary loved her husband and her son. These things filled her heart and her example of motherhood is a fine one to follow.

WORDS FROM WESLEY

Luke 2:16

Holy Ghost, apply Thy word
And promise to my heart,
Tell me I shall see the Lord,
Before I hence depart:
When my faith the Christ hath seen,
Creator of that inward eye,
Thee I shall acknowledge then,
The Lord and God most high.
Spirit of faith, reveal in me
The sure approaching grace,
Then I shall the Deity
Of my Inspirer praise,
Bless my God for ever bless'd,
Glory in salvation given,
Late obtain the promised rest,
And go in peace to heaven. (PW, vol. 7, 247)

When **the shepherds returned** (v. 20), they praised and glorified the Lord for everything they experienced that fateful night. They found the angelic message to be true and they were changed forever.

The good news about Jesus is **for all the people** (v. 10). The story of Christ's birth is a message that can bring salvation to the world. Although this passage is familiar, every time we hear it, it warms our hearts and touches our souls. How wonderful if all the people of the world could experience the advent of Christ in their lives!

DISCUSSION

Taxes! They are about as popular as measles. However, a wonderful event occurred when Joseph, accompanied by Mary, journeyed to Bethlehem to register for taxation. Mary gave birth to Jesus, and the world has never been the same since then.

1. How might God orchestrate political decisions to serve His will?

2. Why was Jesus born in Bethlehem instead of Jerusalem?

3. Do you think it is significant that God first proclaimed Jesus' birth to shepherds? If so, why was it significant?

4. Read John 1:29. Why do you agree or disagree that the shepherds visited God's Lamb in Bethlehem?

5. What aspects of Jesus' birth give you great joy? Why?

6. What actions on the part of the shepherds do you find admirable? Why?

7. How can you share the good news?

8. How might believers glorify and praise God more fully?

PRAYER

Precious Lamb of God, we're awed at the humiliation You endured by entering the world as an infant. Let us serve others with this same humility. Help us reflect Your compassion to a world of people who need Your salvation.

3

LIFE'S GREAT MOMENTS

Luke 2:21–40

Life's circumstances appear in a variety of ways
to show us that God is always at work.

How much potential has God bound into every little bundle of joy? Parents may look adoringly at their baby and wonder if he or she will become a president, prime minister, or pastor. Will that little baby girl's delicate hands eventually cull magnificent melodies from a violin or piano? Is that chunky baby boy destined to become a football or hockey star?

It's fun for parents to speculate, but what really matters is God's will for their child. Praying that God will bless and use their child as He deems best is one of the wisest things parents can do. Mary and Joseph presented Jesus to God in the temple when He was just eight days old.

COMMENTARY

The first two chapters of Luke deal with early stories of Jesus. These chapters are traditionally called Luke's infancy narratives. The grammar in these narratives reflects a Semitic idiom (the verb often comes first in Semitic languages, for example), but the language reflects the style of the Septuagint, the Greek translation of the Hebrew Old Testament, which was used in the early church. It would be much like someone in church today using "thees" and "thous" in their speech. The effect would be to give an Old Testament feel to the narrative. Luke's infancy narratives are largely concerned with the births of Jesus and John the Baptist. In fact, the birth accounts of Jesus and John share many common features. This study is the presentation of Jesus in the temple (Luke 2:21–40). The actual presentation of Jesus (vv. 21–24) is followed by parallel scenes in which Jesus is blessed by contrasting yet complementary male and female characters: Simeon (vv. 25–35) and Anna (vv. 36–40). Luke often narrated male and female parallels.

Circumcision, Naming, and Presentation (Luke 2:21–24)

The circumcision, naming, and presentation of Jesus are parallel to that of John the Baptist (Luke 1:59–80). Biblical scholars have noted over twenty points of comparison. Both stories are reminiscent of the story of Samuel in 1 Samuel 1:22–24.

Luke stated that Mary and Joseph had Jesus circumcised **on the eighth day, when it was time to circumcise him** (Luke 2:21). While the narrative of Acts shows how the gospel goes from Jews to Gentiles, to those outside the Jewish Law, Luke took great care to show how the early Jewish Christians followed the law. The law required that all males be circumcised on the eighth day (Lev. 12:3).

WORDS FROM WESLEY

Luke 2:21

To *circumcise the child*—That He might visibly be *made under the law* by a sacred rite, which obliged Him to keep the whole law; as also that He might be owned to be the seed of Abraham, and might put an honour on the solemn dedication of children to God. (ENNT)

He was named Jesus, the name the angel had given him (Luke 2:21). Naming in Jewish society was significant because it reflected a person's character. The Greek word for Jesus is equivalent to the Hebrew name Joshua, which means Yahweh (the Lord) saves. As Joshua was instrumental in the salvation of the Jewish people during the period of the exodus, so Jesus would be instrumental in their salvation again.

When the time of their purification according to the Law of Moses had been completed, Joseph and Mary took him to Jerusalem to present him to the Lord (v. 22). This again shows the obedience of Jesus' parents to the Jewish Law. Leviticus 12:2–8 states that the mother was ritually unclean for a period of seven days when she gave birth to a male child. Jerusalem figures prominently in Luke's gospel. Luke's gospel begins and ends in Jerusalem. All of Jesus' resurrection appearances in Luke are in Jerusalem. This is in contrast to Matthew's gospel, for example, where the resurrection narratives are set in Galilee.

Leviticus 12:6 requires a year-old lamb and either a pigeon or turtledove for purification. The poor, however, can offer **a pair of doves or two young pigeons** (Luke 2:24), indicating that Jesus' parents were poor. The sacrifice again demonstrates that Joseph and Mary were faithful Jews. Of all the Gospels, Luke in particular expresses greatest concern for the poor.

The Prophecy of Simeon (Luke 2:25–35)

Simeon is described as **righteous and devout** and **waiting for the consolation of Israel** (v. 25). The term **devout** (sometimes translated godly or God-fearing) is used only by Luke in the New Testament (here and in Acts 2:5; 8:2; 22:12). **The consolation of Israel** (Luke 2:25) is not a phrase that occurs in the Old Testament. The term **consolation** is used only one other time in Luke, where the NIV translates it as comfort: "But woe to you who are rich, for you have already received your comfort" (6:24).

Luke further described Simeon in ways that identified him as a prophet. **The Holy Spirit was upon him** (2:25). The Holy Spirit **revealed** things to him (v. 26) and he was **moved by the Spirit** (v. 27). While Luke narrated the outpouring of the Spirit on all Christians in Acts 2, throughout the Old Testament we see examples of prophets or other great leaders who were possessed or empowered by the spirit of the Lord. Thus, we see that David was filled with the Holy Spirit at his anointing (1 Sam. 16:13).

WORDS FROM WESLEY
Luke 2:25

The consolation of Israel—A common phrase for the Messiah, who was to be the everlasting consolation of the Israel of God. (ENNT)

Simeon took Jesus **in his arms and** prayed: **"Sovereign Lord, as you have promised, you now dismiss your servant in peace"** (Luke 2:28–29). **Sovereign Lord** is a single word that is a correlative of *servant* or *slave*. Here we have a picture of manumission: a slave was being released by his master.

"For my eyes have seen your salvation" (v. 30). Most of the occurrences of the word **salvation** in the New Testament occur in Luke and Acts. While salvation sometimes means forgiveness of sins in Luke and Acts, it is often used in a much broader sense.

"A light for revelation to the Gentiles" (v. 32). The Gentile mission drives the narrative of Acts (see Acts 1:8). In Luke's gospel, Jesus came into contact only with Jews, but in Acts the gospel gradually expanded across racial and geographical boundaries. The longest narrative in Acts is the story of the conversion of Cornelius, the first Gentile convert (Acts 10:1 — 11:18). That narrative ends on this note: "So then, God has granted even the Gentiles repentance unto life" (11:18). Acts ends with Paul proclaiming, "I want you to know that God's salvation has been sent to the Gentiles, and they will listen" (28:28). It is difficult for modern Western Christians to understand how radical this idea was, but many conservative Christians in the early church had a hard time accepting Gentiles into the church because they did not follow the Jewish Law. The compromise in Acts 15 and Paul's letter to the Galatians reflect this struggle.

"And for glory to your people Israel" (Luke 2:32). **Glory** typically denotes some visible characteristic that causes people to give honor. Thus a man's glory might be his cattle or his children. God's glory might be described as a pillar of fire or some other visible manifestation.

"This child is destined to cause the falling and rising of many in Israel" (v. 34). What the NIV translates as **this child is destined** literally reads "this one lies." It suggests the placing of an object (Johnson, 55), such as a stumbling stone (see Luke 20:17–18). The life and ministry of Jesus would divide: some would rise, and some would fall.

"So that the thoughts of many hearts will be revealed" (2:35). The prophet is often noted as having the ability to see into a person's heart (Luke 7:39–40).

"And a sword will pierce your own soul too" (2:35). This passage is difficult and has been interpreted in various ways. In the Old Testament, a sword was often used as a symbol of discrimination. One scholar suggests it should be understood that way here: "Simeon hints at the difficulty [Mary] will have in learning that obedience to the word of God will transcend even family ties" (Fitzmyer, 430). Note how Mary is depicted in Luke 8:21 and 11:27–28.

The Prophecy of Anna (Luke 2:36–38)

Anna was Simeon's female counterpart. Anna was a prophet. The NIV translates the term **prophetess** (v. 36), which is simply the feminine form of the word, much like actor and actress. (Language is strange. In certain contexts these feminine forms are slowly falling out of use. The Academy of Motion Picture Arts and Sciences no longer gives an Oscar to the best leading *actress*, but to the best leading *female actor*. It would be difficult to imagine, though, a princess being addressed as a female prince.)

We read about several female prophets in the Old Testament. Miriam, the sister of Moses, was described as a prophet (Ex. 15:20). The most famous female prophet was probably Deborah (Judg. 4:4—5:31). Deborah also was a political leader and one who rendered legal decisions (4:5). Huldah (2 Kings 22:14–20) the prophet functioned very much in a traditional capacity. She delivered an oracle of judgment to the king. The wife of Isaiah was also identified as a prophet (Isa. 8:3).

The primary role of a prophet is that of a preacher. Contrary to the supermarket tabloids, prophets did not typically make long-range predictions such as those attributed to astrologers and alleged psychics. Prophets were preachers who preached to their contemporaries. Theirs were messages of judgment or hope— sometimes both.

Unfortunately, in some Christian traditions, female preachers have been suppressed, largely due to misinterpretation of the New Testament or gender bias. The Wesleyan tradition, though, has historically been supportive of women in ministry, and often in the forefront, understanding that female preachers have been called by God to minister.

Anna was described as a very old saint who had been a widow for many years. **She never left the temple** (Luke 2:37) may be hyperbole. We need not assume she lived in the temple, which would have been unusual. **She never left the temple** may be similar to the expression often used—"We went to church every time the doors were open"—to illustrate faithful church attendance.

Anna, like Simeon, immediately recognized the significance of Jesus. Anna was not simply passively waiting, but was prepared by **fasting and praying** (v. 37). Throughout the Bible as well as throughout history, Christians have prepared themselves to be open to God through fasting and prayer. Anna, like Simeon, spoke about Jesus' significance **to all who were looking forward to the redemption of Jerusalem** (v. 38). The story of Anna ends much like the story of Simeon began. Simeon expected the consolation of Israel, and Anna expected the redemption of Jerusalem.

WORDS FROM WESLEY

Luke 2:38

Let the example of these aged saints animate those, whose hoary heads, like theirs, are a crown of glory, being found in the way of righteousness. Let those venerable lips, so soon to be silent in the grave, be now employed in the praises of their Redeemer. Let them labour to leave those behind, to whom Christ will be as precious as He has been to them; and who will be waiting for God's salvation, when they are gone to enjoy it. (ENNT)

The Trip Back to Nazareth (Luke 2:39–40)

The story of the presentation of Jesus ends with Joseph and Mary returning to their hometown of Nazareth. Again, Luke emphasized that they **had done everything required by the Law of the Lord** (v. 39).

WORDS FROM WESLEY

Luke 2:40

And the child grew—In bodily strength and stature; *and waxed strong in spirit*—The powers of His human mind daily improved; *filled with wisdom*—By the light of the indwelling Spirit, which gradually opened itself in His soul; *and the grace, of God was upon him*—That is, the peculiar favour of God rested upon Him, even as man. (ENNT)

Luke concluded the scene with the statement: **The child grew and became strong; he was filled with wisdom, and the grace of God was upon him** (v. 40). This is again parallel to the concluding statement about John the Baptist: "The child grew and became strong in spirit" (1:80).

References

Joseph A. Fitzmyer, *The Gospel According to Luke I–IX: A New Translation with Introduction and Commentary*. The Anchor Bible, vol. 28 (New York: Doubleday, 1979).

Luke Timothy Johnson, *The Gospel of Luke*. Sacra Pagina Series, vol. 3, ed. Daniel J. Harrington (Collegeville, MN: Michael Glazier, 1991).

DISCUSSION

It has been observed that as the twig is bent so grows the tree. A child is never too young to dedicate to God or to incline toward God's ways.

1. Read Luke 2:21 and Leviticus 12:3. How do these verses help you evaluate Joseph and Mary's regard for God's will?

2. Why do you agree or disagree that publically presenting a baby to the Lord is what Christian parents ought to do?

3. Read Matthew 1:21 and Luke 2:21. Why did Joseph and Mary name the baby "Jesus"? Why is the name Jesus special to you?

4. How does Joseph and Mary's economic status show that God is no respecter of persons?

5. How does Simeon's prayer give you a deep reverence for God?

6. How does it increase your missionary vision?

7. Why do you agree or disagree that elderly preachers can relate to young people?

8. Do you think many Christians are apathetic about the future God has promised? Why or why not?

9. Read Luke 2:40. How can you be "filled with wisdom"?

10. How do you think a person's life will show that the grace of God is upon him or her?

PRAYER

Father, in this study we've seen again Your astounding salvation. Thank You that Your plan included a way for us to experience Your redemption. May we serve You daily as Simeon and Anna did.

4

NO SUCH THING AS CHEAP GRACE

Luke 3:1–18

Prepare your heart to receive Christ.

If you drive across the western states, you may have to dodge tumbleweeds rolling across the road. Tumbleweeds usually travel in clumps, low to the ground. Having broken away from the root, they roll and bump along unanchored at the mercy of the wind.

John the Baptist summoned the people of Israel to exercise genuine faith in the Messiah by sending down roots deep into repentance. Baptism would be meaningless without faith anchored in repentance.

COMMENTARY

At the time John the Baptist began his preaching ministry, God's Spirit had been silent for approximately four hundred years. There had been no prophet sent to God's people in all that time. The people recognized that there was something very different about John. They identified him as a prophet not unlike Isaiah, Jeremiah, or Ezekiel. In fact, his very appearance seems to have resembled the prophet Elijah (see Luke 1:17; Matt. 3:4; 2 Kings 1:8).

John was not sent to the religious hierarchy of his day. Rather, he was sent into the wilderness to preach to the common person. His place of ministry was around the Jordan River—the same river God had brought the nation of Israel across in order to claim the land He had promised them.

John's ministry was multifaceted. He not only preached a harsh message of repentance, but he also preached the gospel or "good news." He taught people of all sorts how to live out their faith. He counseled with those seeking to do God's will.

He was sent as the forerunner of the long-awaited Messiah. John's role was to be a herald. A herald was someone who went before a king to proclaim his entrance into the city and to make sure the road was clear for the king's procession. John understood this role and never overestimated his own importance (John 3:30).

John was a man of courage—courage to speak the Word of the Lord no matter what the cost. As we study this passage, let us remember that we are living in a spiritual wilderness. God wants to send His Word to our hearts so that we too might speak His message to a dying world.

John's Time (Luke 3:1–2)

It was often the custom to begin a historical narrative by dating it according to the contemporary rulers and officials. In these verses, we see that John lived in a real world of real people. Let's examine who some of these people were.

Tiberius Caesar (v. 1) was the Roman emperor who followed Caesar Augustus. He ruled from A.D. 14 through 37. **Pontius Pilate** (v. 1) was the Roman governor. According to Roman history, Pilate was a procurator or prefect, which was a military title of a commander of auxiliary troops. He ruled over Judea from A.D. 26 to 36. **Herod** was the **tetrarch of Galilee** (v. 1). This was Herod Antipas, who ruled over Galilee from 4 B.C. to A.D. 39. Both he and his brother **Philip**, who was **tetrarch of Iturea and Traconitis** (v. 1), were the sons of the cruel Herod the Great. Luke also mentioned **Lysanias tetrarch of Abilene** (v. 1). **Abilene** was north of the other regions mentioned here. **Lysanias** is otherwise unknown.

In addition to political rulers, Luke also mentioned the high priests **Annas** and **Caiaphas** (v. 2). The Jewish Law stated that there was to be only one high priest, from the direct line of Aaron, who was the first high priest, and that this position was held until death. But by this time in Jewish history, the religious system was corrupted, and it was the Roman government that was appointing the religious leaders. It is surmised that Rome deposed Annas, who was high priest from A.D. 6 to 15. His son-in-law Caiaphas took his place and was high priest from A.D. 18 through 36. However, Annas still retained the title of high priest (Acts 4:6) and had power and influence even from the background. Jews would still recognize him as high priest because, according to their law, the position was held until death.

By looking at the dates of these rulers, scholars have surmised that John the Baptist began preaching somewhere between September of A.D. 27 and October of 28.

John's Purpose (Luke 3:3–6)

John's message was **a baptism of repentance for the forgiveness of sins** (v. 3). Baptism was not a new idea to the Jews. For centuries they had baptized Gentile converts in order to rinse away the impurities of their Gentile lifestyle. A bride and groom at the time of their betrothal entered a *mikveh* for a ceremonial cleansing, a sign of their purity before marriage.

WORDS FROM WESLEY
Luke 3:3

By repentance, I mean conviction of sin, producing real desires and sincere resolutions of amendment; and by "fruits meet for repentance," forgiving our brother (Matt. 6:14–15); ceasing from evil, doing good (Luke 3:3–4, 9); using the ordinances of God, and in general obeying Him according to the measure of grace which we have received (Matt. 7:7; 25:29). (WJW, vol. 8, 47)

The baptism John preached about was not for ceremonial cleansing or for washing away of Gentile practices. Rather, it was a sign of repentance. This was a new twist to an old practice. The Jews believed they were clean because of their heritage as descendants of Abraham. They did not believe repentance or this kind of baptism was necessary for a Jew.

John the Baptist did not have a stationary ministry. **He went into all the country around the Jordan** (v. 3). Because baptism was an intricate part of his message, he needed water. The Jordan River stretches seventy miles from the Sea of Galilee to the Dead Sea and had been significant in Israel's history.

But John was not reminding the Jews of their heritage. Instead he was calling them to repentance. To repent means to change your mind and then reorder your life. It is a turning from your sin and a turning to God. It is interesting to note that John connected the terms *baptism*, *repentance*, and *forgiveness*. He was declaring that forgiveness from God was impossible without first turning away from sin.

WORDS FROM WESLEY
Luke 3:5

To rectify my crooked will,
To smoothe my nature's ruggedness,
Reform'd from every outward ill
O bid me now from sinning cease,
Thy way into my heart prepare,
And then display Thy glory there. (PW, vol. 11, 125)

John the Baptist was the fulfillment of what the prophet Isaiah declared. He was **a voice of one calling in the desert** (v. 4). His purpose was to **prepare the way for the Lord** (v. 4). Preparation implies the idea of getting ready for something. After four hundred years of silence, the voice of God resounded not in the sanctified halls of their empty religious practices, but in the wilderness. It was time for Messiah to break onto the scene. And it was important for the people to get themselves ready so that **all mankind** would **see God's salvation** (v. 6). The Messiah would be recognized only by those who would repent and submit to baptism as a sign of their change of heart.

WORDS FROM WESLEY
Luke 3:5

The matter of this sacrament is water; which, as it has a natural power of cleansing, is the more fit for this symbolical use. Baptism is performed by washing, dipping, or sprinkling the person, in the name of the Father, Son, and Holy Ghost, who is hereby devoted to the ever-blessed Trinity. I say, *by washing, dipping, or sprinkling*; because it is not determined in Scripture in which of these ways it shall be done, neither by any express precept, nor by any such example as clearly proves it; nor by the force or meaning of the word *baptize*. (WJW, vol. 10, 188)

John's Message (Luke 3:7–9)

After four hundred years of silence, the message to God's people was not an easy one. As he preached God's message, John said, **"You brood of vipers! Who warned you to flee from the coming wrath?"** (v. 7). This may seem like a harsh message in a day when we are trying to attract people by watering down the gospel message. But God's chosen people needed to be confronted with this truth. The **brood of vipers** he was referring to was the religious leaders. In fact, Jesus used the same term for the Pharisees and Sadducees (Matt. 12:34). Like a snake, they were cunning and full of poison and were leading people away from God rather than to Him.

In his message, John also called for the people to **produce fruit in keeping with repentance** (Luke 3:8). Repentance without deeds to accompany it is worthless. James tells us that faith without deeds is dead (James 2:14–26). The Jews thought their heritage as Abraham's sons guaranteed them access to all of God's blessings. They didn't understand that their lifestyle needed to be in harmony with God's will. Today many attend church and know the "right" words, but, like these Jews, have not committed themselves completely to live for Christ.

WORDS FROM WESLEY
Luke 3:8

Say not within yourselves, We have Abraham to our Father—That is, trust not in your being members of the visible church, or in any external privileges whatsoever: for God now requires a change of heart; and that without delay. (ENNT)

John understood that it was time for the judgment of God. He warned them that **every tree that does not produce good fruit will be cut down and thrown into the fire** (Luke 3:9). Just as in John's day, God is looking for those who produce lives of righteousness, who are obedient to His Word, and who are actively serving Him.

John's Teaching (Luke 3:10–14)

We generally think of John the Baptist as being a prophet—which he was. But his ministry went beyond just declaring God's Word. It was also practical in nature. As the crowds of people came to him, they needed to understand how they could implement these truths. They needed to know how to produce this fruit of repentance. John first told them to share with those who were less fortunate than themselves by giving away an extra tunic or sharing food (v. 11). He was showing them that compassion is an intricate part of a righteous lifestyle.

Tax collectors approached John as well. They had a reputation for being dishonest in their dealings. They would add exorbitant amounts to the taxes due Rome in order to line their own pockets. They were willing to sell out their own countrymen for the sake of a denarius. John's instruction to them was, **"Don't collect any more than you are required to"** (v. 13). This was a radical idea!

Soldiers also approached John. Scholars agree that these were not Roman soldiers, but rather Jewish soldiers whose role was much like that of the police of our day. Just like the tax collectors, they had taken advantage of their countrymen. John's instruction to them was, **"Don't extort money and don't accuse people falsely — be content with your pay"** (v. 14). Obviously greed and power were problems for them. The fruit of repentance demanded that they have integrity in all their dealings with others.

John's Role (Luke 3:15–18)

Because John was recognized as a prophet, it would be easy to see why many began to question whether he was the Messiah (v. 15). Because of the prophetic writings of the Old Testament, the Jews knew that prophecy would accompany the appearing of the Messiah (see Joel 2:28–29; Mal. 3:1).

John knew his role or purpose. He knew his baptism was just an outward sign of the change of heart of the believer. But he also knew that another was coming who would **baptize** them **with the Holy Spirit and with fire** (Luke 3:16). This baptism would be an inward one generated by the Holy Spirit. The prophets looked forward to the coming of God's Holy Spirit, which was promised to the nation of Israel.

In humility, John recognized that his ministry was not about building himself a kingdom, but about building God's kingdom.

He did not own his ministry, but the ministry belonged to the Lord. He knew that the one to come would be greater than he in every way. For he said, **"One more powerful than I will come, the thongs of whose sandals I am not worthy to untie"** (v. 16). In that culture, it was the slave of the household who would remove the sandals and then wash the feet of the guests as they arrived. John saw himself in this role in relation to the Messiah. Likewise, we too should serve God with humility, not building our own ministries or kingdoms, but recognizing that all belongs to the one worthy of our praise.

This prophet recognized that the day had come when God was separating the true believer from the hypocrite. He warned the people that God had **a winnowing fork . . . in his hand** that would **clear his threshing floor and . . . gather the wheat into his barn, but he** would **burn up the chaff with unquenchable fire** (v. 17). **Threshing** was the process of separating the grain of wheat from outer shell or chaff. The **winnowing fork** was used to throw the wheat into the air in order to separate the wheat from the chaff. The **chaff** would then be burned because it was useless.

John was comparing those who refused to repent with the chaff that was burned up. Today God is still looking for people whose hearts are tender toward Him. He is searching for those who have teachable spirits and will confess their sins and have the courage to turn away from their old destructive habits and live for Him.

Today as in John's day, the gospel or **good news** (v. 18) is not a soft message that allows people to do what is right in their own eyes. It is a challenge to stand up and be counted by living righteously and producing fruit that accompanies a heart that has been changed by God's Holy Spirit.

DISCUSSION

God chose John the Baptist to prepare Israel for the arrival of history's most important person, Israel's Messiah.

1. Read Luke 3:1–2. What purpose is served by the historical information given in these verses?

2. How do you know John was commissioned by God to prepare Israel for the Messiah?

3. Do you think it would have been meaningless for the Jews to be baptized without repenting? Why or why not?

4. How did John connect baptism, repentance, and forgiveness?

5. Why do some religious people today say they do not need to repent? How do you respond to such a claim?

6. John preached fearlessly. How can you proclaim sin, judgment, and salvation fearlessly?

7. Why do you agree or disagree that faith and good works are connected?

PRAYER

God, thank You for the example of the selfless ministry of John the Baptist. He pointed to You, Your glory, and Your kingdom. Please take our service and make it equally directed toward building Your kingdom, not ours.

5

LIFE'S GREATEST DECISION

Luke 4:16–24, 28–30; 5:1–11

Our redemption through Christ depends on our response to Christ.

Fishing is a great sport, especially if the fish are biting. There's nothing like carrying a catch of fish home and anticipating what they will taste like after they're cleaned.

Most fishermen have a favorite place and time to catch their gilled prizes, but some days their best fishing efforts go unrewarded. It's never the fishermen's fault, though, they will tell you.

This study relates how Jesus turned a few fishermen's frustrating night of failure into an unprecedented success. Surprisingly, after hauling in mounds of fish, they decided to walk away from it all and follow Jesus. We, too, must decide that following Jesus is life's most important decision.

COMMENTARY

In Luke 3, Jesus was baptized by John. This was the beginning of Christ's ministry. In a sense, it was like His ordination. He did not need the approval or authority of others, but this event served as the initiation for His ministry.

Next, Jesus was tempted by the Devil in the wilderness for forty days. Jesus overcame the Tempter through His knowledge and use of the Word of God and prayer. When His time of trial was completed, Christ went to His hometown of Nazareth, empowered by the Holy Spirit. It is in this context that this study is set. As we progress through the passages at hand, we want to focus on the contrasting ways in which people responded to Jesus.

Jesus Rejected at Home (Luke 4:16–24, 28–30)

Jesus must have been excited to preach in His hometown. Luke 4:14–15 tell us that news about Him spread throughout the land and many people spoke well of Him. So Jesus **went** home **to Nazareth** (v. 16), a small town in Galilee. It was there that the angel Gabriel spoke to Joseph and Mary about the conception and ministry of Jesus. Nazareth was "home," and Jesus went to church **on the Sabbath . . . as was his custom** (v. 16). This may have been Jesus' home church. There is something special about the church in which we grow up. We have many memories there and lots of loving and kind people who invested in our lives.

Notice that it was Jesus' custom to attend church. Some people cannot attend church regularly on Sabbath days because their occupations keep them away. These people find great blessing in attending services on other days of the week. Unfortunately, some people are out of the habit of attending church at all.

Jesus **stood up to read** (v. 16). In the Jewish service, there is a time for reading the Scriptures. Jesus may have been handed the scroll for the day's reading. The passage Jesus read was part of His mission on earth—to preach the gospel. The passage He read and His comment on it had a powerful effect on those who heard Him.

Many people interpret the groups mentioned to be spiritual in nature. It was to the "spiritually poor" that Jesus preached. The prisoners were "spiritual prisoners." The blind people were "spiritually blind." The year of the Lord's favor was a spiritual one. Others interpret the passage more literally.

Jesus recognized that the **Spirit of the Lord** (v. 18) was upon Him. One thing the world needs more of today is anointed preaching. The benefits of such a preacher on a congregation and community are enormous. Solid biblical preaching produces strong laypeople. It bolsters our faith. It encourages our hearts. It convicts us of sin. It points us to the Savior. It builds cumulative biblical knowledge. There are so many positives to strong preaching that they cannot be listed here. Pray for your pastor and his or her preaching ability. Ask the Holy Spirit to anoint the preacher as he or she speaks for Him. Eternity hangs in the balance.

Jesus knew He was anointed to preach, and so He began at His home church. His message would be one of hope for many people. **The poor** (v. 18) would hear good news. What is good news for poor people? Good news is the hope of help and better days ahead. The gospel is spiritual food for those who are spiritually hungry. Christ said in John 4:32, "I have food to eat that you know nothing about." Christ's audience may have thought, "That's alright; good for the poor people, but I am not poor." They may not have understood it to be a reference to themselves.

WORDS FROM WESLEY

Luke 4:18

He hath anointed me—With the Spirit. He hath, by the power of His Spirit which dwelleth in me, set me apart for these offices. *To preach the gospel to the poor*—Literally and spiritually.

How is the doctrine of the ever blessed Trinity interwoven, even in those scriptures where one would least expect it? How clear a declaration of the great Three-One is there in those very words, *The Spirit*—of the *Lord* is upon *Me!* (ENNT)

Jesus said He was **sent . . . to proclaim freedom for the prisoners** (Luke 4:18). At some point in our lives, we are all prisoners of sin. Hebrews 12:1 says, "Let us throw off everything that hinders and the sin that so easily entangles, and let us run with perseverance the race marked out for us." The depths and reaches of sin and depravity are everywhere today. People in all walks of life on every continent are in need of deliverance. Jesus is the great Deliverer!

The blind (Luke 4:18), too, have hope through Jesus. He said they would recover their sight. It's hard to imagine the joy of seeing after being blind for many years. Bartimaeus must have given thanks every day for the rest of his life. Our vision is one of the most important senses we have. We can survive without it and even prosper as did Fanny Crosby, for example. However, Jesus' message is to those who are spiritually blind. He will open their eyes, and they will see a whole new world filled with love, joy, peace, patience, kindness, goodness, faithfulness, gentleness, and self-control. It is a world that is brighter and more joyful than any other entity on earth.

WORDS FROM WESLEY

Luke 4:23

Ye will surely say—That is, your approbation now outweighs your prejudices. But it will not be so long. You will soon ask, Why my love does not begin at home? Why I do not work miracles here, rather than at Capernaum? It is because of your unbelief. Nor is it any new thing for me to be despised in my own country. So were both Elijah and Elisha, and thereby driven to work miracles among heathens, rather than in Israel. (ENNT)

The oppressed (v. 18) will be released from their suffering. Entire nations suffer oppression at the hands of ruthless dictators. Churches and church people suffer oppression from legalistic and domineering leaders. Spouses and children suffer oppression from abuse in their homes. Women and children suffer oppression through human trafficking. Jesus promised that those who are oppressed will one day be set free. If not in this life, then certainly in the next.

WORDS FROM WESLEY

Luke 2:24

I who so oft have seen
The tokens of Thy power,
Vilest and sinfulest of men,
O how shall I adore!
Struck by Thy piercing eyes,
Unclean in lips and heart,
I fall; and all my nature cries
"From me, O Lord depart!"
Before Thy holiness
Shall I presume to' appear,
When purest angels hide their face,
And tremble to draw near?
What fellowship with light
Can darkness e'er maintain,
Or how shall sinners in Thy sight,
Or at Thy feet remain?
When Thou appear'st below
Thou show'st me what I am,
My darkness by Thy light I know,
And suffer all my shame;
Abash'd I see and feel
The vast disparity,
The distance inconceivable
Betwixt my God and me!
Yet Thou my Saviour art,
Whose love transcends the sky,
And canst not find it in Thy heart
To leave and let me die;
Whilst after Thee I mourn,
Thou wilt not let me faint,
But stay a sinful man to turn
Into a sinless saint. (PW, vol. 5, 142–143)

The year of the Lord's favor (v. 19) is a reference to the Year of Jubilee in the Old Testament. It occurred every fiftieth year and called for the restoration of property and the cancellation of debts. Interestingly enough, Jesus' model prayer includes the phrase "forgive us our debts [trespasses] as we forgive our debtors [those who trespass against us]." Imagine the hope a message like this would have been to people in those conditions.

Perhaps the people in the congregation were thinking, "That's fine, but it doesn't apply to me. I'm not poor, blind, in prison, or oppressed." Jesus meant the message for them and applied it to them in the next verses.

Their response was one of anger and wrath. They **were furious** (v. 28) at Jesus and sought to kill Him. Taking **him to the brow of the hill**, they wanted **to throw him down the cliff** (v. 29). That must have been one powerful sermon! The Bible says Jesus **walked right through the crowd and went on his way** (v. 30). The Father had more ministry for Jesus, and His time had not yet come.

Let's take a moment and think about what happened. Jesus spent time fasting and praying in the wilderness and returned in the power of the Holy Spirit. He read some Scripture and preached a bit in His home church, and they became furious and tried to kill Him.

Their response to **Joseph's son** (v. 22) is a reflection of what was in their hearts. They were in need of transformation. They were filled with hatred and anger. Their spirits were oppressed, and they did not even realize it. They were blind to the person of Jesus. They saw Him only as the illegitimate child of Joseph and Mary. They were in spiritual poverty and enjoyed feeding on the husks around them instead of partaking of the Bread of Life. Instead of experiencing the greatest year of their lives, a year of divine favor, they pronounced judgment on themselves by their own actions.

Their lack of faith was something Jesus did not change. They rejected His person as the Son of God. They rejected His authority as a minister. They rejected His anointing as a preacher. They rejected His ministry, feeling they did not need it. Jesus came unto His own, and His own received Him not.

It is sad but true that many people today still reject Jesus. Our task is to tell them. They have to decide whether to believe in Him.

WORDS FROM WESLEY
Luke 4:28

And all in the synagogue were filled with fury—Perceiving the purport of His discourse, namely, that the blessing which they despised, would be offered to, and accepted by, the Gentiles. (ENNT)

Peter and Others Left All to Follow Jesus (Luke 5:1–11)

These verses stand in contrast to the response by the people in Nazareth. Jesus called Peter to leave his successful fishing business and follow Him. Peter walked away from it and followed Jesus.

The Lake of Gennesaret (v. 1) was also known as the Sea of Galilee. Jesus spent much of His ministry in towns around the shores of this body of water. It lay about seven hundred feet below sea level and was fed by the Jordan River and springs in the lake bed. Its deepest point was about 150 feet. It was well-stocked with fish and subject to violent storms that arose quickly.

Jesus was speaking there on the shore, and a large crowd of people were listening. Desirous of aiding the crowds, Jesus looked for a boat from which to speak. He saw two with fishermen washing their nets. Jesus stepped into Peter's boat, and they pushed out from shore so that the crowds would have more room and Jesus could continue teaching. It must have been quite a sight for the crowds to see Jesus teaching from the boat.

Perhaps as a favor for the use of his boat, Jesus asked Peter to **"put out into deep water, and let down the nets for a catch"** (v. 4).

Peter replied by calling Jesus **Master** (v. 5) and stating that although they had **worked hard all night and** caught nothing, because of Peter's great respect and admiration for Jesus, he would do as he was asked.

Verses 6–7 record a catch of fish so large that Peter's nets began to break. There were so many fish that it took both boats to haul them in. This was perhaps the single greatest catch of Peter's life and that of his partners — James and John.

Peter was so astonished by the catch that he fell to his knees and confessed his sins by saying, **"I am a sinful man!"** (v. 8). Note that before the catch, Peter referred to Jesus as **Master** (v. 5); after the catch, He was **Lord** (v. 8). This is a completely different response to Jesus than that of the people at Nazareth! In Nazareth, Jesus was neither Master nor Lord. He was "Joseph's son." Peter was a sinner, and the people of Nazareth were sinners too. The difference was faith. Peter believed, and the people of Nazareth did not.

Jesus called Peter to stop catching fish and begin catching people (v. 10). Verse 11 records that **they** — Peter and his partners, James and John — **left everything and followed** Jesus.

It is amazing that these men walked away from the greatest catch of their careers. Their business had just experienced the single best day they had ever had, yet at the word of Christ, they left it all behind and followed Jesus. God calls us all to follow Him. He calls us all to leave some things behind. He calls us all to be fishers of men, women, and children.

Perhaps this is a good time to hear the words of our Savior in verse 10: **"Don't be afraid."** It is scary to leave everything we know that is familiar and step out in faith into the unknown. However, when we see Jesus as Lord, our lives are transformed into the men and women He would have us to be. We then are willing to become His disciples and if need be leave all and follow Him.

DISCUSSION

What is life's greatest decision? Choosing a college major? Choosing to pursue a certain line of work? Choosing to get married? Choosing to buy a house? Choosing to have children? Actually, life's greatest decision is none of these. It is the decision to believe in Jesus as Savior.

1. Read Luke 4:18–19. In what sense are unbelievers poor, imprisoned, blind, and oppressed?

2. How can you minister to the people just described?

3. Why might it be hard for a preacher to be accepted in his or her hometown?

4. Read Luke 4:28–30. How do you explain the fact that religious people can become hateful and even murderous?

5. Read Luke 4:38–41 and 5:1–3. What do you think caused so many people to clamor for Jesus' teaching?

6. Based on your reading of Luke 5:3–11, what commendable traits do you see in Simon Peter?

7. Which of your possessions have you made available to Jesus? Why should believers regard the Lord as the owner of all they possess?

8. Can there be "good fishing" where your church is located? Why or why not?

9. How can you become a more effective soul winner?

PRAYER

Jesus, we ask You to be more than "Joseph's son," to us. We need You as Savior, Lord, and Master. So, wherever You send us, we will go. Whatever sacrifice You ask of us, we will make willingly.

6

HEALING FAITH

Luke 7:1–10; 8:42–48

To be healed, we must bring our needs to God.

An injury or serious illness saps our energy, but it may also sap our faith. "Why me?" we may ask. "Why did God let this happen to me?" Usually, our faith is challenged even more when a loved one or close friend suffers.

At such times, we can criticize and doubt God or pour out our hearts before Him. When a Roman centurion was deeply concerned about one of his most valued servants who had become terminally ill, he did the right thing. He asked Jesus to heal the servant. The response was positive. Jesus healed the servant without even entering the centurion's house.

This study will help you roll your burdens onto Jesus' shoulders.

COMMENTARY

Luke, the author of the third gospel, was a doctor in addition to being an evangelist who accompanied Paul on a number of his missionary journeys. As such, we might expect that he would have had a keen interest in the accounts he heard from the apostles of Jesus' healing ministry. This study includes two of those accounts: that of healing a centurion's servant and that of healing a woman with a bleeding disorder. Both accounts point out the importance of faith in the healing process.

In addition to being a doctor, Luke was also a Gentile. Early church historians Jerome and Eusebius say Luke was from the city of Antioch in Syria. The recipient of his gospel, as well as

Acts, was also a Gentile named Theophilus, likely a wealthy government official in Antioch. Luke took special care in his writing to show that the ministry and message of Jesus were not only to the Jewish people, but to Gentiles as well.

Much of Jesus' public ministry was devoted to healing people of various physical and spiritual disorders. Sickness was present in the world as a consequence of the fall of Adam and Eve. Jesus, however, announced that He had come to "proclaim freedom for the prisoners and recovery of sight to the blind, to release the oppressed, to proclaim the year of the Lord's favor" (Luke 4:18–19; see Isa. 61:1–2). Healing people was a sign that He had come from His Father in heaven, and that His Father's heart was one of love. It was also a demonstration of the fact that He had come to defeat the works of Satan and reverse sin's curse.

Jesus Healed a Centurion's Servant (Luke 7:1–10)

The events of Luke 7 follow immediately after Jesus selected His twelve disciples and delivered a sermon to a large crowd. The sermon, as recorded by Luke, has many similarities to the Sermon on the Mount found in Matthew 5–7, but is believed by many scholars to be somewhat different and is referred to as the "sermon on the plain." When Jesus had finished preaching, **he entered** the village of **Capernaum** (Luke 7:1). This city served as a kind of "home base" for Jesus and His disciples while He ministered in Galilee. And even though Galilee was not formally occupied by the Romans, it had a garrison of Roman soldiers located in Capernaum.

Jesus' reputation for being a healer had already spread widely among the citizens of Galilee (see 6:17–19). When He arrived in Capernaum, He was met by some Jewish elders of the city who came to Him on behalf of a God-fearing centurion who was stationed there. A centurion was an army officer in charge of a hundred Roman soldiers. He was likely the son of a Roman senator or another powerful figure who was beginning his career at that level. Roman soldiers were especially hated by the Jewish people because they were an occupying force of an oppressive and brutal pagan empire. But this centurion apparently did not fit that mold. The elders appealed to Jesus on his behalf because he loved their nation and built their synagogue.

Luke included the accounts of three significant Roman centurions in his gospel and the book of Acts, and in each case, he presented them in a positive light. In addition to the centurion whose servant was healed, Luke mentioned one who stood near the cross at Jesus' crucifixion and commented, "Surely this was a righteous man" (Luke 23:47). In Acts, he told the story of a centurion named Cornelius who was a God-fearer (Acts 10:24–48). He, along with all those who were gathered in his home, received an outpouring of the Holy Spirit in their midst similar to that at Pentecost, which demonstrated to Peter and the apostles that the gospel must be made available to the Gentiles as well as the Jews.

The appeal of the centurion to Jesus was not for himself, but on behalf of one of his servants. He valued this man very highly, in spite of the fact that he was only his servant. The historian Josephus recorded that Roman soldiers often had many servants who trained and even fought with them. This one was possibly his own personal attendant to whom he had grown much attached. Unfortunately, he was very ill and close to death. Matthew's account indicates that he was paralyzed and suffering terribly (Matt. 8:6). Jesus decided to go with them to his house.

Before they got there they were met by a contingent of the centurion's friends who had been sent with another appeal. Perhaps the centurion was aware of the Jewish custom forbidding a Jew from entering a Gentile home, and to ask a rabbi to do this would have made him unclean. So this time, the centurion made his appeal to Jesus' authority. As an army officer, he understood authority, for he himself obeyed the orders given to him, and in turn, he gave orders to those under him. So rather than having Jesus come to his home in person, he asked that Jesus would simply give the order for his servant to be healed. He understood that Jesus' words had power and authority in them. Perhaps he was even aware of the psalm that said, "He sent forth his word and healed them; he rescued them from the grave" (Ps. 107:20).

WORDS FROM WESLEY
Luke 7:6

Yet, being in doubt, whether "the high and lofty One that inhabiteth eternity" will regard such a sinner as him, he wants to pray with those who know God, with the faithful, in the great congregation. But here he observes others go up to the table of the Lord. He considers, "Christ has said, 'Do this!' How is it that I do not? I am too great a sinner. I am not fit. I am not worthy." After struggling with these scruples awhile, he breaks through. And thus he continues in God's way, in hearing, reading, meditating, praying, and partaking of the Lord's Supper, till God, in the manner that pleases Him, speaks to his heart, "Thy faith hath saved thee. Go in peace." (WJW, vol. 5, 199)

Luke records that **when Jesus heard this, he was amazed at him** (7:9). One might expect that one of the disciples who had witnessed any of Jesus' other healing miracles might possibly have responded with a similar kind of faith, but even they did not have the courage to make a request like that. Here was one who was a Gentile, one without the advantages of being educated in the Law and the Prophets, one who was outside of the covenant community of Israel, and his expression of faith surpassed anything Jesus had witnessed to that point. The centurion knew, without a doubt, that Jesus had the power and authority to do even the impossible. And that faith both amazed and pleased Jesus.

Luke never said whether Jesus ever actually did speak the word commanding the servant's healing, but he did indicate that when the centurion's friends returned to his house they found the servant completely healed. Matthew wrote that "his servant was healed at that very hour" (Matt. 8:13), or immediately. It seems apparent in this instance, from Jesus' commendation of the centurion's faith, that faith played some role in the servant's healing. And the faith in question was not that of the one who was healed, but of the one who appealed to Jesus on his behalf. His faith, Jesus implied when He remarked that He had not seen **such great faith even in Israel** (Luke 7:9), should serve as a model for all.

Jesus Healed a Bleeding Woman (Luke 8:42–48)

While still ministering in Galilee, Jesus was once again met by a crowd of people. His reputation and popularity among the people was gaining in strength. In that crowd was a ruler of the local synagogue by the name of Jairus, who had a daughter who was very ill, near death. He pleaded with Jesus to come to his home and heal her. So the crowd followed, anticipating that they might possibly be witnesses to a miracle. **As Jesus was on his way, the crowds almost crushed him** (v. 42).

WORDS FROM WESLEY

Luke 8:42

But it may well be thought a thing incredible, that *man* should raise the dead; for no human power can create life. And what human power can restore it? Accordingly, when our Lord (whom the Jews at that time supposed to be a mere man) came to the house of Jairus, in order to raise his daughter from the dead, upon the first intimation of His design, "they laughed him to scorn." "The maid," said He, "is not dead, but sleepeth." "This is rather to be called sleep than death; seeing her life is not at an end; but I will quickly awaken her out of this sleep."

However, it is certain, she was really dead, and so beyond all power but that of the Almighty. But see what power God has now given to man! To His name be all the praise! (WJW, vol. 7, 135)

Among the many people in the crowd was a woman who had been suffering for twelve years. She had a disease that resulted in constant bleeding, most likely a menstrual or uterine disorder. According to Mark's gospel, she had been treated for all those years by a number of doctors, but to no avail. She had even spent all the money she had on those doctors. Her malady was both embarrassing as well as socially ostracizing. According to the Levitical law (Lev. 15:25–33), she lived in a constant condition of ceremonial uncleanness and was thereby excluded from worship in the synagogue. Not only so, but she would not have been able to have any normal social relationships, because anyone who touched her would also become ceremonially unclean. Had the crowd known she was there, or been aware of her condition, she would undoubtedly have been treated very unkindly.

WORDS FROM WESLEY

Luke 8:43

How vain our strife to heal
The plague incurable!
Still the plague remains unstay'd.
Still the issue is undried;
Reason's philosophic aid
Heightens, and inflames our pride.
Endeavouring to restrain,
The law augments our pain:
Virtue's firm resolve we boast,
Boast our liberty of will;
All our confidence is lost,
Cannot stop the raging ill.
The' original disease
Our medicines but increase:
Happy when at last we know
Human insufficiency,
When we truly humbled go,
Jesus, for relief to Thee. (PW, vol. 11, 173)

Because of her condition, this woman was desperate, so she worked her way through the very full crowd until she could finally reach out her hand and touch the edge of Jesus' cloak. She believed, as did many people, that the clothes of a holy man somehow imparted spiritual and healing power (Mark 6:56; Acts 19:11–12). She also likely believed that if Jesus was aware of her unclean condition He might not have wanted to touch her himself. So she risked the danger of elbowing her way through the crowd until she finally got close enough. And when she did touch His cloak, **immediately her bleeding stopped** (Luke 8:44) and she was healed!

Jesus was aware that something had happened. He stopped in His tracks and asked the crowd, **"Who touched me?"** (v. 45). Everybody denied it, in spite of the fact that almost everyone close to Him had undoubtedly bumped and jostled Him all along the way. His disciple Peter even recognized that fact and pointed it out to Him. Jesus' question actually sounded a bit absurd to those around Him. Nevertheless He was aware that somewhere along the way, spiritual power had actually gone out from Him. That does not mean His power had been diminished, as if it were a kind of consumable commodity. It did mean, though, He was aware that someone in the crowd had tapped into the limitless power of the Holy Spirit that He bore within himself.

The woman knew she could not remain unnoticed any longer, so she **came trembling and fell at his feet** (v. 47). She would undoubtedly be exposed for having, in her unclean and diseased state, come into the crowd and exposed the others, particularly a rabbi, to her uncleanness. She was probably frightened of Jesus' response, as well as that of the crowd. But that didn't matter anymore. She had been healed! The bleeding had stopped. So when she identified herself before Jesus and the crowd, she heard him speak those beautiful words: **"Daughter, your faith has healed you. Go in peace"** (v. 48).

WORDS FROM WESLEY

Luke 8:48

I went to Mr. Sims's, in expectation of Christ. Several of our friends were providentially brought thither. We joined in singing and prayer. . . . I rose at last, and saw Mr. Chapman still kneeling. I opened the book, and read aloud, "And, behold, a woman, which was diseased with an issue of blood twelve years, came behind him, and touched the hem of his garment: for she said within herself, If I may but touch his garment, I shall be whole. And Jesus turned him about, and when he saw her, he said, Daughter, be of good comfort; thy faith hath made thee whole. And the woman was made whole from that hour." My heart burned within me, while I was reading: at the same time I heard him cry out, with great struggling, "I do believe." We lifted him up; for he had not power to rise of himself, being quite helpless, exhausted, and in a profuse sweat. An old believer among us owned himself affected with a wonderful sympathy. We had the satisfaction of *seeing* Mr. Chapman increase in faith; and returned most hearty thanks to the God of his and our salvation. (JCW, vol. 1, 112)

There were times in Jesus' ministry when He healed people as a direct response to their faith. There were times when He healed in response to the faith of those around the sick people. And there were even times when He healed people where faith was never mentioned. There does not appear to be any exact formula for healing in Scripture. In this particular instance, it seems that Jesus himself did not directly heal the woman. His Father allowed His power to flow into the woman and provide healing for her sickness in response to her faith gesture of reaching out and touching His garment.

It was not Jesus' clothing that healed her. It had no magical powers in it. No object has that power. Jesus said that her faith had healed her. She showed faith by reaching out to the only one who could heal her. Faith in itself does not heal. It must be placed in the right person. And in speaking of her faith, Jesus called the woman **daughter** (v. 48). She came to Jesus for healing, but she left with a relationship and peace with God.

DISCUSSION

Even highly successful men and women face challenges. For example, their health or the health of a loved one may decline and bring them near death. But no challenge is too difficult for the Lord to handle.

1. Why do you agree or disagree that the Roman centurion risked losing respect and perhaps even his military rank by seeking Jesus' help?

2. Read Luke 7:5. Why do you think the centurion loved the Jewish people?

3. How does Jesus' consent to help the centurion's servant broaden your understanding of His mission?

4. Read Luke 7:6–8. How do the centurion's actions and words set an example for you?

5. How do you explain the fact that Jesus found the centurion's faith so amazing (v. 9)?

6. How did the centurion's servant suddenly become well?

7. Read Luke 8:42–48. How was the incident of healing described in this passage so unique?

8. Why doesn't every believer who is critically ill or infirm get healed? Should we attribute the lack of healing to absence of faith or to the will of God? Explain.

9. Why do you agree that it takes strong faith to endure a physical infirmity for an extended period?

PRAYER

Father, in Jesus' name we ask You to increase our faith so we may learn to ask lavishly and expect Your gracious, powerful response to our prayers. Give us faith that we may please You.

7

HUMBLY I BOW

Luke 7:36–50

Humility and love flow from a life transformed by God's forgiveness.

A couple from Virginia mingled with guests, including the vice president, during President Obama's first state dinner in late November 2009. They even were photographed with dignitaries. Their attendance created quite a stir, though, because they had not been invited. Somehow, they had managed to pass through security and blend in because they looked like they belonged.

This study focuses on a woman who crashed a dinner Jesus was attending. She didn't look like she belonged. Far from it, but she poured out her devotion to Jesus and received His commendation and forgiveness. We need to accept misfits—even outlandish sinners—and help them find Jesus' forgiveness.

COMMENTARY

Jesus' early ministry took place mostly in the region of Galilee, which was home to himself and most of His disciples. He called Peter, James, and John away from a life of fishing for fish in order to fish for people. He called Matthew away from his materialistic career of collecting taxes. In all, He chose twelve men to follow Him as His disciples (Luke 6:12–16). In the days that followed, He taught them about the nature of the kingdom of God and went from one town to another teaching the crowds and healing people of various diseases.

There were two radically different responses of the people to Jesus' ministry. A number of people, especially those who came from a sinful past, were eager to embrace His message of grace. John the Baptist had gone before Him and announced the coming of the kingdom. Many, especially sinners, came and were baptized by John, acknowledging that "God's way was right" (Luke 7:29). "But the Pharisees and experts in the law rejected God's purposes for themselves" (7:30). They thought John's message didn't apply to them, and Jesus' offer of grace toward sinners actually nullified the law. Consequently, they were constantly critical of both His actions and message.

The Pharisees were a Jewish sect in Jesus' day that had a particular obsession with the law, more specifically the oral law. Along with most Jews of their day, they accepted the Mosaic law as inspired and authoritative. But alongside the Mosaic law, they also regarded as authoritative all of the explanatory and supplementary material, the oral tradition, which had developed during the period of Babylonian exile. It came to be revered so highly that it was said to go back to Moses himself. Detailed exposition of the law appeared in the form of highly specific injunctions that were designed to "build a hedge" around the written Torah and guard against any possible infringement of it. The result was hundreds of laws that were not contained in the Torah itself.

The Pharisees were passionate about living a righteous life. For that, they must be commended and even admired. Sadly, they believed righteousness could be obtained only by observing every minute detail of the law. This legalistic rigor of the Pharisees could be seen in Jesus' day by their tithing of herbs (Matt. 23:23; Luke 11:42), the wearing of conspicuous phylacteries and tassels (Matt. 23:5), the careful observance of ritual purity (Mark 7:11), frequent fasting (Matt. 9:14), distinctions in oaths (23:16), and so forth. Unfortunately, the sheer weight of these laws made it impossible for anyone to obey them all, and that resulted in Jesus' frequent condemnation of the Pharisees as hypocrites. Their rigorous concern for external matters to the neglect of the more important matters of the heart brought about sharp denunciations by Jesus in His later ministry.

Not all of the Pharisees in Jesus' day opposed Him, though. Nicodemus was a Pharisee and even a member of the Sanhedrin who sincerely sought out Jesus in order to inquire about spiritual matters (John 3). Joseph of Arimathea was also presumably a Pharisee who, along with Nicodemus, sought the body of Jesus in order to give it a respectful burial (John 19:38–42). Gamaliel, Paul's teacher, warned the Jewish ruling council not to rush to judgment in respect to Jesus, believing that if He truly was from God, they could not thwart Him, but if He was not then God would ultimately bring His work to an end.

Jesus Was Anointed by a Sinful Woman (Luke 7:36–38)

The Pharisees had accused Jesus of being a "glutton and a drunkard, a friend of tax collectors and 'sinners'" (Luke 7:34). Shortly after Jesus had given an invitation to Matthew to become one of His disciples, Matthew held a banquet where he invited all of his tax collector friends to come and meet Jesus. That really upset the Pharisees, who believed that truly righteous people ought to separate themselves from those who had no real concern for the law. In their minds, Jesus seemed to spend most of His time hanging around people whom they regarded as sinners. But it was sinners that Jesus indicated He came to seek and save (Luke 19:10). At Matthew's party, He even told the critical Pharisees, "It is not the healthy who need a doctor, but the sick. I have not come to call the righteous, but sinners to repentance" (5:31–32).

Jesus was not one to discriminate against people—not even Pharisees. Not only did He eat with tax collectors and sinners, but He even accepted an invitation from a Pharisee named Simon to join him for a dinner in his home. It was an elegant, formal meal where the guests all **reclined at the table** (7:36). In this position, they would lie on couches with their heads near the table, propping themselves up on one elbow and stretching their feet out behind them. Usually, before doing so, they would also remove their sandals, and their feet would be washed by servants.

WORDS FROM WESLEY

Luke 7:36

And one of the Pharisees asked him to eat with him — Let the candour with which our Lord accepted this invitation, and His gentleness and prudence at this ensnaring entertainment, teach us to mingle the wisdom of the serpent, with the innocence and sweetness of the dove. Let us neither absolutely refuse all favours, nor resent all neglects, from those whose friendship is at best very doubtful, and their intimacy by no means safe. (ENNT)

But there was also an uninvited guest at this meal. **A woman who had lived a sinful life in that town learned that Jesus was eating at the Pharisee's house** (v. 37), and she decided to invite herself. **She brought** with her **an alabaster jar of perfume** (v. 37). A meal like this was not a private affair, as people would often come in, sit along the edges, and listen to the conversation. But this woman's reputation preceded her. She was known throughout the community for her sinful lifestyle. She may likely have been a prostitute. She certainly would not have been welcome in this particular company. She should not be confused with the woman who also anointed Him with perfume at Bethany during His last week with the disciples (Mark 14:1–9; John 12:1–8).

This woman came to Simon's home on a mission. She came near to where Jesus was, and then **stood behind him at his feet weeping** (Luke 7:38). She felt great sorrow on account of her sin. Perhaps she had already found forgiveness through listening to Jesus' preaching or through the ministry of John the Baptist and now wanted to show her gratitude. In any event, her tears began to fall on His feet, and **she wiped them with her hair** (v. 38). Then, taking the alabaster flask of perfume from around her neck, she broke it and poured it out on His feet. This was not a onetime act, though, for the verb tense indicates that she kept kissing His feet and putting perfume on them. And as the perfume's fragrance filled the room, she was no longer unnoticed by those in attendance.

Simon Reacted to the Woman's Actions (Luke 7:39)

As Simon the Pharisee became aware of what was taking place, he began to stew within himself. Jesus was a holy man, a rabbi. Any self-respecting rabbi would have realized this woman's sinful nature and recoiled at being touched by her. As a sinner, she was regarded as "unclean," and she would have made anyone she touched unclean. Pharisees avoided any contact whatsoever with "uncleanness." Surely Jesus would have known who and what kind of woman she was.

Simon had no concern with the woman's plight. He had no desire to help her find healing or redemption. Instead, he simply judged her as a sinner and wanted nothing to do with her. He was more concerned with maintaining his own righteousness and reputation than with her soul.

Jesus Taught Simon about Forgiveness (Luke 7:40–43)

Even though Simon never voiced his feelings, Jesus knew exactly what he was thinking (see also Luke 5:22; 6:8). He always does. And self-righteousness was one thing He never seemed to let pass. So He told Simon He had something to tell him. Politely, Simon agreed to listen, and Jesus told him a parable.

The parable focused on a moneylender and two of his creditors. One of the creditors owed the moneylender a great deal of money—five hundred denarii. A denarius was equivalent to a whole day's wages, so this man owed the better part of two full years' wages. The other man owed the lender just fifty denarii. But neither of the men had the means to pay the lender back. Rather than consigning them to slavery on account of their debts, though, the moneylender instead generously canceled the debts of both men.

WORDS FROM WESLEY
Luke 7:40

And Jesus said, Simon, I have somewhat to say to thee—So tender and courteous an address does our Lord use even to a proud, censorious Pharisee! (ENNT)

After telling this short story, Jesus posed this question to Simon: **"Which of them will love him more?"** (7:42). The point was too easy to miss, and Simon begrudgingly responded, **"I suppose the one who had the bigger debt canceled"** (v. 43). Seeing that he had understood His point, Jesus acknowledged to him that he had judged correctly.

Jesus Forgave the Woman's Sins (Luke 7:44–50)

After telling Simon the parable about the moneylender and the creditors whose debts had been forgiven, Jesus turned toward the woman and drove His point to Simon home. Simon may not have committed any grievous breach of the law of Moses, but he had committed several social errors in the short time Jesus had been with him. For one, he had neglected to wash Jesus' feet, which a host or one of his servants was always expected to do, because sandaled feet got very dirty. Second, he did not offer Jesus a kiss of greeting, a courtesy generally extended to guests. Finally, he did not anoint His head with oil. By contrast, the sinful woman had washed His feet with her tears, kissed His feet, and anointed Him with expensive perfume—and she was not even the host!

WORDS FROM WESLEY

Luke 7:44

Thou gavest me no water—It was customary with the Jews, to show respect and kindness to their welcome guests, by saluting them with a kiss, by washing their feet, and anointing their heads with oil, or some fine ointment. (ENNT)

Jesus continued His point: **"Her many sins have been forgiven—for she loved much. But he who has been forgiven little loves little"** (v. 47). She demonstrated by her humility and acts of love that she had been forgiven. But she was not forgiven because of her love; she was forgiven because of her **faith** in Jesus (v. 50). So Jesus turned to her and spoke the most beautiful words any sinner could ever hope to hear: **"Your sins are forgiven"** (v. 48). Simon, on the other hand, who felt he had very little in his life that needed God's forgiveness, had little love to show for it. In fact, his judgmental spirit showed quite the opposite.

WORDS FROM WESLEY

Luke 7:47

Those many sins of her's are forgiven; therefore she loveth much—The fruit of her having had much forgiven. It should carefully be observed here, that her love is mentioned as the *effect* and *evidence*, not the *cause* of her pardon. She knew that much had been forgiven her, and therefore she loved much. (ENNT)

Jesus' words of forgiveness to the sinful woman did not sit well with Simon's other guests (presumably also Pharisees). They were keenly aware that only God has the power and authority to forgive sins, so by speaking those words, Jesus had actually put himself on par with God. They or some of their friends had had a similar discussion on the same topic when Jesus had healed a paralyzed man some time before this (Luke 5:20–21). Instead of recognizing who He really was, as the woman did, they chose instead to question His right to forgive sins.

But Jesus was not yet finished. He also said to the woman, **"Your faith has saved you; go in peace"** (7:50). The Pharisees, who sought righteousness in their performance of keeping the law, never experienced it. The sinful woman, on the other hand, who put her faith in Jesus, went away from the dinner fully justified and at peace. Jesus' life and ministry demonstrated over and over again that righteousness is obtained only through faith in God, not through works.

DISCUSSION

We can imagine how we would feel if we were at a party and an unwelcomed person crashed it. But think if you were that party crasher—desperate for any chance to praise Jesus. Reflect on that feeling of desperation, thinking of the last time you felt that deep need to talk to Him.

1. Read Luke 7:36. Are you shocked that a Pharisee would invite Jesus to dinner? If so, why?

2. How would you react if a homeless man with the smell of liquor on his breath asked you to take him to lunch? Would you see this as an opportunity to tell him about Jesus? Why or why not?

3. How do you think the sinful woman, the party crasher, obtained the alabaster jar of perfume?

4. Read Luke 7:44–46. How did the woman's sacrificial act contrast with the treatment Simon showed Jesus?

5. Why do you agree or disagree that some people are "too far gone" for God to save?

6. Why do you agree or disagree that the more aware a person is of his or her sins the more he or she appreciates forgiveness?

7. The sinful woman showed her love for Jesus in a tangible way. How will you show your Savior that you truly love Him?

PRAYER

Father, too often we've been like Simon—self-righteous and insensitive to the way You are at work in others' lives. Help us gain Your perspective of ourselves and others so we can love and serve You more faithfully.

8

THE POWER OF LOVE

Luke 9:51–56; 10:29–37

Love breaks down walls of animosity and hatred.

Apparently, there was no love lost between George Bernard Shaw and Winston Churchill. On one occasion, Shaw sent Churchill two theater tickets with the note: "I am enclosing two tickets to the first night of my new play; bring a friend . . . if you have one."

Such animosity has often existed not only between individuals, but also between races. For example the Jews and the Samaritans held centuries-old hatred for one another. But Jesus opposed hatred and prejudice. He told a pious Jew a story about a good Samaritan who rescued a severely wounded traveler at great personal cost. The Samaritan truly obeyed the law to love his neighbor as himself.

This study challenges our love for our "neighbor."

COMMENTARY

The Scriptures for this study introduce a new phase of Jesus' earthly ministry. Except for occasional visits to Jerusalem to attend feasts (Feast of the Passover in John 2:13 and again in John 5:1), the first two years of Jesus' ministry were spent in and around Galilee. Very early before He began His public ministry, He went to Bethabara east of the Jordan River to be baptized by John the Baptist (Matt. 3:13) and was then immediately led by the Spirit into the wilderness of Judea, where He was tempted by the Devil (Matt. 4:1–11). He returned to Galilee, where He began His public ministry. Soon thereafter, John recorded that He made the trip to Jerusalem for the Passover; cleansed the temple of money changers the first time; had the encounter with Nicodemus; and got the attention of the Pharisees, who heard that Jesus' disciples were baptizing more people than John (John 2:13— 4:1). Apparently, Jesus didn't feel it was right to oppose the Pharisees so early in His ministry, so He went back to Galilee for almost two years of ministry.

Jesus and the Samaritans (Luke 9:51–56)

On the trip from Jerusalem to Galilee, Jesus had His first recorded encounter with the Samaritans at Sychar (John 4:4–42). His interaction with the Samaritan woman at the well and the openness of the people of Sychar to His message stand in sharp contrast to the way He and His disciples were received two years later when He left Galilee to go back to Jerusalem to begin His Judean ministry (Luke 9:51). Jesus had chosen to travel through Samaria rather than take the longer route east of the Jordan south to Jerusalem in order to avoid Samaria. He sent some of His people on ahead to arrange food and lodging, presumably James and John, but they ran into trouble—**the people there did not welcome him, because he was heading for Jerusalem** (v. 53). And herein lies a long story.

WORDS FROM WESLEY

Luke 9:51

He steadfastly set his face—Without fear of his enemies, or shame of the cross. (ENNT)

When King Solomon died, his son Rehoboam became king. The northern tribes refused to accept him as king, and they crowned Jeroboam instead. War ensued, but Rehoboam was not able to retain control over the northern tribes; the kingdom was divided into two parts. The northern kingdom became known as Israel with its capital in Samaria, and the southern kingdom became Judah with Jerusalem as its capital. Yet in spite of the division, even the northern tribes still looked to Jerusalem as the holy city and sought to return there often to worship.

The Assyrians conquered Samaria in 721 B.C. and took many of its inhabitants into captivity (2 Kings 17:24). The king of Assyria then resettled the kingdom with many nationalities and religions. Religious mayhem ensued. The result was that "they worshiped the LORD, but they also served their own gods in accordance with the customs of the nations from which they had been brought" (2 Kings 17:33). When the Jews returned to Jerusalem after the Babylonian/Persian captivity, they refused to allow the Samaritans to help them rebuild the temple (Ezra 4:1–4; Neh. 4:1–3, 7).

The old antagonism between the north and the south developed into open enmity between the two groups. The Samaritans built a rival temple on Mount Gerizim and declared the five books of Moses as the only Scriptures and Moses as the only prophet. Animosity was deep and abiding and was still a problem in the days of Jesus' ministry. At the time of the verses for this study, Samaria was a territory with nebulous boundaries between Galilee and Judea. And even though it made the trip longer and more arduous, Jews traveling between Galilee and Judea usually took the longer route east of the Jordan rather than travel through Samaria. And the Samaritans made it very difficult for any Jews traveling through their territory toward Jerusalem. Some sense of the degree of animosity comes out in the response of **James and John** when they wanted to **call fire down from heaven to destroy them** (Luke 9:54). Jesus rebuked them rather severely, saying, "You do not know what manner of spirit you are of. For the Son of Man did not come to destroy men's lives but to save them" (vv. 55–56 NKJV).

The fact that this attitude was troubling to Jesus gave rise very soon to an opportunity to reinforce His love for the Samaritans.

WORDS FROM WESLEY
Luke 9:54

Vengeance doth to God belong:
Who the mind of Jesus have,
Kindness we return for wrong,
Only wish our foes to save.
If to Christ in spirit join'd,
If in us His bowels move,
Anger at the *sin* we find,
More than life the *sinner* love.
Let the furious sons of *Rome*
Show exterminating zeal,
Loathsome heretics consume,
Call for fire from heaven—or hell:
Lord, in their behalf we call,
Send Thy Spirit from above,
Burn their sins, consume them all,
Burn their souls with fire—of love. (PW, vol. 11, 189–190)

The Good Samaritan (Luke 10:29–37)

"Good Samaritan" was an oxymoron to most Jews, including the disciples, but Jesus wanted to break down those walls built by centuries of animosity and hatred.

The occasion arose one day while Jesus was teaching. A lawyer stood up and asked Jesus, rather insincerely, "Teacher . . . what must I do to inherit eternal life?" (v. 25). Probably he emphasized the "I" in his question, because even after quoting Deuteronomy 6:5 and Leviticus 19:18 like a good student of the law, he still wanted to justify himself. Evidently he didn't want Jesus to expound further on the subject of loving God, but he asked, **"And who is my neighbor?"** (Luke 10:29). That was when Jesus hit him with "both barrels." He told him a story.

A man was going down from Jerusalem to Jericho, when he fell into the hands of robbers (v. 30). This road was probably the best-known road to the listening audience. It drops about thirty-six hundred feet in the seventeen miles between the two cities. Apparently it was very dangerous and frequented by robbers and bandits. No surprise to the people that Jesus chose this setting for His story. Like all good robbers (another oxymoron), **they stripped him of his clothes, beat him and** left **him half dead** (v. 30). Again, no surprises.

WORDS FROM WESLEY

Luke 10:30

By the love of our neighbour, I mean universal benevolence; tender good-will to all men. For in this respect every child of man, every son of Adam, is our neighbour; as we may easily learn from our Lord's history of the good Samaritan. (WJW, vol. 10, 155–156)

A priest happened to be going down the same road (v. 31). Of course, here is the "neighbor." Certainly a priest, seeing his Jewish brother lying bloody and beaten, will help him! After all, that's what priests do! But he didn't even slow down: **when he saw the man, he passed by on the other side** (v. 31). But the lawyer had an answer, we can surmise. The priest couldn't afford to make himself unclean, because he was on his way to minister at the temple. Or he'll pray for him at the temple today. No great surprise here.

So too, a Levite, when he came to the place (v. 32). Ah, certainly this good layman is the "neighbor." He's used to blood—he works in the temple assisting the priests with sacrifices. Surely he will stop and help the poor man. But surprise, surprise, the Levite merely went over, took a look at the beaten and bloody man, and **passed by on the other side** (v. 32). Now that's a surprise! If neither the priest nor the Levite would help, what hope is there for the poor man? What could Jesus possibly be getting at with all this?

But a Samaritan, as he traveled, came where the man was; and when he saw him, he took pity on him (v. 33). We can begin to understand the lawyer's predicament. He was suddenly caught in the web of his own conceit. One can almost see him shrinking before the gaze of the Master: A Samaritan, a neighbor? They are not even . . . persons! But watch what happened: the Samaritan **went to him and bandaged his wounds**; he poured **on oil and wine** to sooth and to heal. Then he inconvenienced himself by putting the wounded **man on his own donkey, took him to an inn and took care of him** (v. 34). The Samaritan saw a man in need, not a Jew. He saw a fellow human being who was hurting, and he did what he could to help him, sharing freely of his time and resources.

The next day he took out two silver coins (v. 35), enough to pay for the man's care for up to two months by some estimates. He instructed the innkeeper to take care of the man and said, **"When I return, I will reimburse you for any extra expense you may have"** (v. 35). The Samaritan may have been known to the innkeeper, having traveled that way frequently, or the innkeeper may have decided, "Anyone who shows that kind of love and compassion, Samaritan or not, is all right in my book!"

Which of these three do you think was a neighbor to the man who fell into the hands of robbers? (v. 36). Jesus turned the question back to the lawyer, who had to give some kind of an answer. **The expert in the law** had to reply, **"The one who had mercy on him"** (v. 37). How did Jesus apply the story? He said, **"Go and do likewise"** (v. 37). The next time you see a person hurting and in need, go to that person and take care of him or her. The next time you meet a "Samaritan" say, "Hello, neighbor!"

WORDS FROM WESLEY

Luke 10:37

And he said, He that showed mercy on him—He could not for shame say otherwise, though he thereby condemned himself and overthrew his own false notion of the neighbour to whom our love is due. *Go and do thou in like manner*—Let us *go and do likewise*, regarding every man as our neighbour who needs our assistance. Let us renounce that bigotry and party zeal which would contract our hearts, into an insensibility for all the human race, but a small number whose sentiments and practices are so much our own, that our love to them is but self-love reflected. With an honest openness of mind let us always remember that kindred between man and man, and cultivate that happy instinct whereby, in the original constitution of our nature, God has strongly bound us to each other. (ENNT)

That kind of love will break down walls of animosity, hatred, and prejudice that divide. That kind of love will make us one in Christ. We can assume that James and John and the rest of the disciples also got the point!

This parable broke down walls of hatred the Jews had for the Samaritans and vice versa. However, there are other applications that show the love God has for sinful man:

- **Down from Jerusalem** (v. 30)—the direction of all humankind without hope.
- Robbed, **stripped**, and beaten (v. 30)—the condition of humans under Satan's power.
- **Half dead** (v. 30)—by nature left twice dead, dead in trespasses and sins, utterly unable to help ourselves.
- **Passed by on the other side** (vv. 31–32)—the law could not give relief and hope; literally passed by on the other side with no power to save.
- **A Samaritan . . . took pity on him** (v. 33)—God sent His Son in the likeness of sinful flesh to condemn sin in the

flesh (see Rom. 8:3). The law of the Spirit of life in Christ Jesus has made us free from the law of sin and death!

* **Bandaged . . . wounds, pouring on oil and wine** (Luke 10:34)—Jesus came to where wounded, lost, sinful humankind lay by the side of the road, took on himself the likeness of sinful humanity, yet without sin, and gave himself as a ransom, redeeming, saving, and healing us by His own precious blood (1 Pet. 1:19); "to him who loves us and has freed us from our sins by his blood" (Rev. 1:5).

* **Took him to an inn and took care of him** (Luke 10:34)—what a blessing to be cared for by the Lord! Cast all your cares on the Lord who cares for you (1 Pet. 5:7).

* **Look after him** (Luke 10:35)—He literally "paid the price." And when Jesus went away, He said "I will not leave you comfortless. I will send another comforter to guide you into all truth" (see John 14:16–17). He also established the church to guard and care for the flock.

* **When I return** (Luke 10:35)—Jesus said, "I go to prepare a place for you, that where I am there you may be also" (see John 14:1–3). He will come again.

"Then I saw a Lamb, looking as if it had been slain. . . . And they sang a new song: 'You are worthy to take the scroll and to open its seals, because you were slain, and with your blood you purchased men for God from every tribe and language and people and nation. You have made them to be a kingdom and priests to serve our God, and they will reign on the earth'" (Rev. 5:6, 9–10).

DISCUSSION

Racial prejudice causes ill will between individuals and even tears at the fabric of a nation. Both the Old and New Testaments report cases of racial prejudice and teach emphatically that God loves all people and wants them to know and love Him.

1. Why would Jesus "resolutely set out for Jerusalem" (Luke 9:51), knowing His life would be in danger there?

2. Have you ever felt unwelcome away from home? What was the occasion? How did you feel?

3. Read Luke 9:54–55. What do the contrasting attitudes reported in this passage reveal about Jesus and His two disciples, James and John?

4. Why do you agree or disagree that racial prejudice contradicts what the Bible teaches?

5. Have you ever felt the sting of discrimination? If so what was the occasion, and how did you respond?

6. Read Luke 10:30. The man journeying from Jerusalem to Jericho was traveling downhill. How might this downhill course picture the human race's journey since sin entered the world?

7. Read Luke 10:31–32. How do you think organized religion sometimes fails needy sinners?

8. What might it cost an individual or a congregation to be "good Samaritans"?

9. Why do you agree or disagree that a church should care for people in the community who are hurting not only spiritually, but also physically, emotionally, and mentally?

PRAYER

Lord God, we don't want to be like a proud Pharisee who avoids contact with hurting people who are our neighbors. Make us attentive to needs around us. Please equip us to serve them in Your love and grace.

9

WHAT A FRIEND WE HAVE IN JESUS!

Luke 10:38—11:13

Followers of Jesus Christ must know how to nurture
a love relationship with God.

Take time to be holy," an old hymn advises. Perhaps we need
the admonition more now than ever before. In spite of a host of
laborsaving devices, we seem to find less time to spend in God's
Word and prayer. We rush through breakfast, perhaps grabbing
a pastry and a cup of coffee. Occasionally we skip lunch in order
to complete an important project. After work, we may settle for
microwave dinner so we can get the kids to soccer practice or
music lessons. By nighttime, we are too busy with household
chores, homework, church meetings, or community events to take
time to be holy.

This study shows that we must choose to take time to be holy.

COMMENTARY

Luke gives us a series of truths about discipleship starting in
9:57–62, which is about the *cost* of discipleship. From 10:1–24, we
learn about the *ministry* of discipleship through Christ's disciples.
In 10:25–27, Luke gives us an *example* of discipleship. In this
study, we focus on the *priorities* and *prayer* of discipleship.
Both are woven together with a relationship with Jesus. Without
a personal relationship with Him, the teachings of these passages
cannot be fully understood.

One Thing Is Needed (Luke 10:38–42)

On His way to Jerusalem to die for the sins of the world, Jesus stopped at Bethany and the home of His friends—Mary, Martha, and Lazarus—for strength and support. Martha, the first to greet Him, busied herself in serving the best the home could provide. Her sister chose to spend time with Jesus rather than focusing on other tasks of service and hospitality.

●

WORDS FROM WESLEY

Luke 10:39

And therein St. Paul undoubtedly alluded to Mary sitting at the Master's feet. (Luke 10:39) Meantime, Martha was *cumbered* with much serving: was *distracted, dissipated.* . . . It is the very expression from whence St. Paul takes the word which we render, *without distraction*.

And even as much serving dissipated the thoughts of Martha, and distracted her from attending to her Lord's words, so a thousand things which daily occur are apt to dissipate our thoughts, and distract us from attending to His voice who is continually speaking to our hearts: I mean, to all that listen to His voice. We are encompassed on all sides with persons and things that tend to draw us from our centre. Indeed, every creature, if we are not continually on our guard, will draw us from our Creator. The whole visible world, all we see, hear, or touch, all the objects either of our senses or understanding, have a tendency to dissipate our thoughts from the invisible world; and to distract our minds from attending to Him who is both the Author and End of our being. (WJW, vol. 6, 445–446)

Martha, frustrated with her sister's seeming lack of concern for the job at hand, suggested to Jesus, **"Don't you care that my sister has left me to do the work by myself?"** (v. 40). Jesus saw through the dynamics of the dilemma and calmed Martha by identifying her problem—she was **worried and upset about many things** (v. 41). The answer to her condition was to concern herself with **one thing** (v. 42).

That **thing** was to sit at the feet of Jesus and listen to Him (v. 39). God created us all with different personalities and temperaments. Some people are more action-oriented, while others are more contemplative. Both types of people are needed and useful in the kingdom. Martha was trying to serve the Lord in her own strength, when she needed to spend some time developing her relationship with the guest in her home, Jesus.

Once we invite Jesus into our lives, we are responsible for developing our relationship with Him. This is best done through quiet times in Bible reading and prayer. The more time we spend with our Lord, the more we will grow spiritually. We begin to like the things He likes and think like He thinks. We become more like Him as we learn more about Him. Our service for the Lord should spring out of our overflowing love for Him. To serve Him is a good thing, especially when we are "whole."

Martha was worried and troubled. She needed spiritual help, and Jesus could provide it if she would take the time to sit at His feet.

WORDS FROM WESLEY

Luke 10:42

To recover our first estate from which we are fallen is the one thing needful: to re-exchange the image of Satan for the image of God, bondage for freedom, sickness for health! Our one great business is to erase out of our souls the likeness of our destroyer, and to be born again, to be formed anew after the likeness of our Creator. This is our one concern, to shake off this servile yoke, and regain our native liberty; to cast away every chain, every passion, that does not accord with an angelical nature. The one work we have to do is to return from the gates of death, to have our diseases cured, our wounds healed, and ourselves restored to perfect soundness. (SCW, 81)

How often do we miss the grace of God because we are too busy doing good things, even important things? How often have we acted first and prayed later? For sure, there is a time to act and a time to wait. Each of us must determine which is appropriate for us at any given point. Martha missed her cue.

But before we get too negative about Martha, we must remember that some people may use their spirituality as an excuse not to get involved in ministry. They are too busy praying and studying the Bible. They may have become too heavenly minded to be any earthly good. Somewhere in the middle is the place God wants us to be. Serving Him from an empty heart can be counterproductive. Never serving Him with a full heart can be self-destructive. We must spend sufficient time in Bible reading and prayer to make us sensitive to the needs of others and ourselves.

Teach Us to Pray (Luke 11:1–4)

The request posed by the disciples is an interesting one, considering their religious culture. They said to Jesus, **"Teach us to pray, just as John taught his disciples"** (v. 1).

John's disciples were easily identified by their prayers. When they prayed, the things they said and the way they said them were such that all who heard them knew they were associated with John.

The disciples wanted everyone to know they were associated with Jesus. They wanted a special prayer that would identify them as His followers and disciples.

These men already knew how to pray. It was the Jewish custom that all males twelve years old and older were to participate in the morning and evening prayers of the community. So, each of these men probably grew up praying with their fathers twice daily. They knew how to talk to God. They knew the Old Testament passages about prayer. They also knew there was something different about Jesus' prayers. His prayers were personal and sounded like a man talking to his father. They wanted to have the intimacy with God that Jesus had.

Let us look at Jesus' model prayer. It is interesting to note that the record of this prayer in Matthew is longer than it is here. Both prayers are the same, except Luke's is shorter, omitting some of the last lines. Luke did this because he was writing to a primarily Gentile audience. Matthew was writing to a primarily Jewish audience, so he used the longer version as they were familiar with the prayers of temple worship.

WORDS FROM WESLEY

Luke 11:2

We may observe, in general, concerning this divine prayer, First, that it contains all we can reasonably or innocently pray for. There is nothing which we have need to ask of God, nothing which we can ask without offending Him, which is not included, either directly or indirectly, in this comprehensive form. Secondly, that it contains all we can reasonably or innocently desire; whatever is for the glory of God, whatever is needful or profitable, not only for ourselves, but for every creature in heaven and earth. And, indeed, our prayers are the proper test of our desires; nothing being fit to have a place in our desires which is not fit to have a place in our prayers: What we may not pray for, neither should we desire. Thirdly, that it contains all our duty to God and man; whatsoever things are pure and holy, whatsoever God requires of the children of men, whatsoever is acceptable in his sight, whatsoever it is whereby we may profit our neighbour, being expressed or implied therein. (WJW, vol. 5, 332–333)

When Jesus said **Father** (v. 2), He was breaking new ground. This is the first time anyone had referred to God so intimately. In the Old Testament, God is referred to as a Father but not as "our Father" (see Matt. 6:9). We might even pray to Him as "my

Father." The word *our* is more corporate in nature and signals to us that this is a prayer to be prayed in public.

Your kingdom come (Luke 11:2) and "your will be done" (Matt. 6:10) are the same things. For God's kingdom to come is to have His will done. It is helpful for us to pray for God's will to be done in our lives from time to time. This is comforting and also a reflection of our dependence on God, especially when we are experiencing difficulties or tragedies.

Give us each day our daily bread (Luke 11:3). We are to ask God for and trust Him to provide for us the necessities for daily living. Sometimes we concern ourselves too much with the future, when it would be helpful to live one day at a time. Much anxiety and emotional turmoil is a constant companion of those who have not learned to live one day at a time. Manna was provided for the day, and only on the eve of the Sabbath was enough given for two days. Look to heaven for your needs today, and trust Him for what lies ahead.

Forgive us our sins, for we also forgive everyone who sins against us (v. 4). This is a conditional statement. Jesus wants us to ask forgiveness for our sins, but also to forgive others. If we refuse to forgive others, can we realistically expect God to do for us what we will not volitionally do for someone else? No, we cannot expect that. The good news is this: With the help of God, we can forgive others. To forgive someone is to release the clutches that hinder our prayers. Today, forgive that one who has sinned against you, so that you can enjoy times of refreshing from the Lord.

Lead us not into temptation (v. 4). Jesus wants us to get into the habit of praying for spiritual strength. God has promised to provide a way of escape from temptation when we ask Him and look for a way out (see 1 Cor. 10:13).

Persistence in Prayer (Luke 11:5–13)

This story is about a man who had nothing to serve his guests, so he went to his friend's house at midnight and asked for help. His friend refused because he didn't want to awaken his family. It was common in those days for the family to sleep together in one bed (v. 7). Often, their homes had few rooms, and for him to get up in the night would mean rousing some of the light sleepers in the home.

We might contrast this request with Martha's busyness. Both of these people wanted to provide for their guests. It was culturally unacceptable to have guests and provide them nothing to eat. Hence, Martha was worried, and this man was asking for help at midnight. So what's the difference? Martha's busyness in preparing the meal kept her away from Jesus, and this man's continual request is an analogy of persevering prayer. Martha was too busy to pray and this man was busy praying.

Eventually, the friend gave him **bread** (vv. 5, 8) so that the pounding at the door didn't awaken his family. God wants us to come to Him in our time of need and ask for His help. This man's need was genuine and sincere, but unlike God, his friend was reluctant in meeting his need. God is not reluctant but eager and invites us to come to Him so He can meet our needs.

Some things we will only receive from God if we pray for them. God is like a father who gives good gifts to His children. Our prayers to Him are a reflection of our trust in Him to provide for us what is good. Sometimes God answers with "no." When He does so, we can be sure He has our best interests in mind, even if we cannot understand it at the time.

Notice the progression is verse 9: **ask . . . seek . . . knock**. The point here is to keep at it until you see results or have a definite answer (v. 10). It may also imply putting feet to our prayers or praying about a matter and trying to accomplish it with God's help. The Bible says in James 4:2, "You do not have, because you do not ask God." How many blessings have we missed because of our lack of asking?

When we do not know how to pray, God inspires us through the yearnings of our souls. There are at least three ways to learn how to pray. First, we learn how to pray by reading the prayers of others. These may be the prayers in the Bible or prayer book. Second, we learn how to pray by listening to the prayers of others. Third, we learn how to pray by actually praying—just do it! The more we pray, the easier it is to pray. In fact, there is a sense in which our whole lives are permeated with and by prayer. The Bible says in 1 Thessalonians 5:17 to "pray continually." That means to offer prayers throughout the day as they are needed and helpful both for ourselves and for others.

The greatest gift God wants to give us, His children, is His **Holy Spirit** (Luke 11:13). The Holy Spirit is the one who empowers, teaches, comforts, guides, convicts, and anoints us. He is God's immediate presence in our lives. In all your asking, ask God to give you His Holy Spirit. He is God's presence in this world today.

Is there any reason why you wouldn't make more effort to develop your relationship with God? Will you spend more time in prayer throughout your day? Will you reprioritize your life so that you can get to know God better? Will you sit at Jesus' feet?

WORDS FROM WESLEY

Luke 11:13

As He expresses himself on another occasion, including all good things in one, "How much more shall your heavenly Father give the Holy Spirit to them that ask him?" (Luke 11:13). It should be particularly observed here, that the persons directed to ask had not then received the Holy Spirit: Nevertheless our Lord directs them to use this means, and promises that it should be effectual; that upon asking they should receive the Holy Spirit, from Him whose mercy is over all His works. (WJW, vol. 5, 190–191)

DISCUSSION

BFF is a term that shows up in social media, especially in correspondence by young people. It means Best Friends Forever. Jesus is every Christian's BFF. Reflect on how you can deepen your friendship with Jesus.

1. Why do you agree or disagree that Mary and Martha had totally different personalities?

2. Does a person undergo a complete personality change when he or she becomes a believer? Why or why not?

3. How might a believer today sit at Jesus' feet?

4. Read Luke 10:40. Why was Martha upset with Mary? Did she have a right to be upset? Why or why not?

5. How might a woman feel if she were extremely active in church work, whereas others did nothing? How should she feel?

6. How can you choose to sit at Jesus' feet in such a busy, busy world?

7. Why do you agree or disagree that the need to pray is increasing as our culture shifts further away from Christian values?

8. How might a church create a greater interest in personal prayer? In public prayer?

PRAYER

God, we want to bring You glory through our actions, words, and thoughts. We want to forgive others as You forgave us. We want to depend on You to meet our needs. Help us grow in these areas.

10

THE PARABLE OF THE LOVING FATHER

Luke 15:11–32

_____

Returning to a loving relationship with the Father is
always a reason to celebrate.

Kidshealth.org reports there are between one million and three
million runaway and homeless kids living on the streets in the United
States. Most runaways occur because of family problems. A divorce,
the arrival of a stepparent, abuse, or drugs are just a few of the many
reasons kids run away from home. Unfortunately, running away
from home usually leads to even bigger problems on the streets.

This study zeroes in on a young man who left home because
he wanted to "live it up." He learned later that his decision
brought disastrous results. So he returned home as a humble and
repentant son. This study portrays the love and forgiveness our
heavenly Father extends to everyone who returns to Him.

COMMENTARY

The heart of the gospel message lies in God's offer of grace
and forgiveness to all humankind. In his fifteenth chapter, Luke
retold three parables of our Savior that highlight the initiative
God takes to redeem and restore the lost. Jesus told these stories
in response to the criticism of the teachers of the law and Pharisees
regarding His personal interaction with "sinners" and tax collectors.
Throughout these parables, the stark difference between the attitude
and approach of the religious leaders with the attitude and
approach of God is a dominant feature.

For the sake of purity, the Pharisees and teachers of the law
sought to avoid interaction with those who did not fully keep the

law. One could not be the guest of these "sinners" nor have them as guests. They expected God to one day judge and destroy those who did not keep the law, and they would rejoice if that were to take place.

In contrast, Jesus presented a God who cares for all who are "lost." First, He told about a shepherd who left behind ninety-nine sheep to find one that was lost. Upon finding the sheep, he called his friends and neighbors to celebrate the recovery of this precious animal. Jesus said heaven rejoices more over one sinner who repents than ninety-nine righteous keepers of the law.

In the second parable, Jesus told of a woman who lost a silver coin, equivalent to a full day's wage. Unwilling to give up on her lost coin, she swept the floors and turned her home upside down until she found the coin. Once again, friends and neighbors were called to celebrate the discovery of that which was lost.

God is not out to destroy the disobedient, but to win them back: "For the Son of Man came to seek and to save what was lost" (Luke 19:10).

The Rebellious Son (Luke 15:11–16)

Jesus prepared to address the objections of the Pharisees and teachers of the law by introducing a father with two sons. The father in the parable clearly represents God. Of the two sons, the older son is not immediately introduced. It is the younger one who first speaks, saying, **"Father, give me my share of the estate"** (v. 12). This initial request for his part of the estate demonstrates the irresponsibility of the younger son. He was not thinking about what was best for the future or what was best for his father. A father might pass on an inheritance before death, but in so doing the father placed himself at the mercy of the child. This son had no interest but his own pleasure. In spite of the boy's intentions, the father granted him his portion. According to the law, the younger son would have received a third of the estate

(Deut. 21:17). If the son was determined to go his own way, the father would let him go. The best hope for his son was to give him the freedom to learn his lessons the hard way.

WORDS FROM WESLEY

Luke 15:12

Give me the part of goods that falleth to me — See the root of all sin! A desire of . . . of independency on God! (ENNT)

With money in his pocket, the young man wasted little time saying good-bye. He **got together all he had, set off for a distant country and there squandered his wealth in wild living** (Luke 15:13). Far from home, the son cast off all restraint and went wild. He lived purely for the moment, carelessly spending his inheritance with no thought for tomorrow. With nothing to limit his sprees, he used up all of his financial resources. And it just so happens, **there was a severe famine in that whole country, and he began to be in need** (v. 14).

This young man had never known need. He was raised in the comfort of his father's estate and lived it up as long as his inheritance allowed. With food scarce and no money in his pocket, he was forced to find employment. His new boss sent him into the fields to feed the pigs. The hunger pangs in his stomach were so strong he found the pods or husks that the pigs ate appealing. To his dismay, no one would give him even a single husk to eat (v. 16). This inability to find any relief for his hunger pangs demonstrates the depths to which sin can take us. Sin lures us in with promises of happiness and satisfaction. In the end, however, sin's promises prove to be false. The final consequence of rebellion is complete emptiness and misery.

●

The Lost Son Returned Home (Luke 15:17–21)

After reaching the lowest point of his life, the son **came to his senses** (v. 17). Through his pain and loneliness, he realized the life he wanted could not be found in a life of sin. Far better was life in his father's house. He remembered the abundance of food that even the day laborers enjoyed in his father's employ. While he was starving to death, the least person who worked for his father filled his belly and had food left over.

Realizing the error of his rebellion, the prodigal announced, **"I will set out and go back to my father and say to him: Father, I have sinned against heaven and against you"** (v. 18). The son had changed. His pride had been replaced with complete humility. He was truly repentant. He made no attempt to cover up his sin, but openly confessed the wrong he had done against heaven and his father. Not only was he sorry for his past violations, but he was eager to chart a new course. To continue to pursue his wayward path would be as foolish as it would be destructive. The far better decision was to place his life at the mercy of his father. The psalmist made a similar conclusion: "Better is one day in your courts than a thousand elsewhere; I would rather be a doorkeeper in the house of my God than dwell in the tents of the wicked" (Ps. 84:10).

The lost son began the journey home to his father. **But while he was still a long way off, his father saw him and was filled with compassion for him; he ran to his son, threw his arms**

around him and kissed him (Luke 15:20). The father did not wait for the son, but ran to meet him. While this activity sounds natural enough to us today, by the norms of Jewish culture, the father would have stayed put. The proper approach would be for the son to come to the father and demonstrate the respect his father was due before making his request. With this unusual action, Jesus emphasized the grace and forgiveness of the Father. Just as a shepherd seeks a lost lamb and a woman seeks a lost coin, the Father seeks lost souls. When we come to our senses and repent, the Father stands eager to embrace us. So full of compassion is He that He showers us with His affection.

Before the father began party preparations, the son came clean with a full confession. With a contrite heart, he admitted sinning against heaven and his father. Because of his actions, the son believed he was no longer worthy of any claims to sonship (v. 21). He did not expect things to ever be as they were before he left home. He was no longer deserving of the honor of being a son of the owner.

The Father Threw a Party to Celebrate (Luke 15:22–24)

The father quickly brushed aside the son's insistence on being a servant. Instead, he ordered, **"Quick! Bring the best robe and put it on him. Put a ring on his finger and sandals on his feet. Bring the fattened calf and kill it. Let's have a feast and celebrate"** (vv. 22–23). His rags were removed from his back and replaced with a luxurious robe. The family ring settled once more on his finger. Brand-new sandals added comfort to his weary feet. And since slaves did not wear shoes, the sandals also indicated his freedom. A choice calf fattened up for just such a special occasion was killed, and the party was started. The object of the feast was to celebrate the return home of the son who **was dead and is alive again; he was lost and is found** (v. 24). The rebellious and wayward son had come home. If all heaven rejoices at the return home of one sinner, it's time to party.

WORDS FROM WESLEY
Luke 15:23

Let us be merry—Both here, and wherever else this word occurs, whether in the Old or New Testament, it implies nothing of levity, but a solid, serious, religious, heartfelt joy: indeed this was the ordinary meaning of the Word two hundred years ago, when our translation was made. (ENNT)

The theme of joy is repeated in verses 7 and 10, as well as verses 23–24. To those who would prefer God smite all sinners, Luke painted a different portrait. God is a benevolent and loving heavenly Father. He is a God who longs to be reunited with all who repent of their sins. He offers grace freely to any who turn to Him from their wicked ways. All of the effort required in searching for the lost becomes worth it when just one responds.

The Older Brother Objected (Luke 15:25–32)

While the party kicked into gear, the older son remained in the field. He was ever faithful to his duties. Hearing the noise of the party, he asked one of the servants what was taking place. **"Your brother has come," he replied, "and your father has killed the fattened calf because he has him back safe and sound"** (v. 27). Surprisingly, this news did not elicit joy in the older brother. Although he had not seen his brother for some time, there were no smiles or tears of gladness. In contrast to the forgiving attitude of his father, the son chose not to release his brother from his sins (v. 28). He refused to go to the party, so his father came out to the field to beg him to join the celebration. Seething with anger, the older brother needlessly reminded his father that he had been the dutiful son who had always obeyed. He had been the one who faithfully slaved in the fields while **this son of yours** (v. 30; not "my brother") was out wasting his inheritance on **prostitutes**. Furthermore, he accused his father of giving special treatment to his younger brother. In spite of all his efforts, his father had never thrown a party in his honor. He had never killed even as much as a young goat on his behalf, yet the younger brother got the royal treatment and a **fattened calf**.

The father responded tenderly, saying, **"My son . . . you are always with me, and everything I have is yours"** (v. 31). While the son saw his years of service as bondage, the father saw them as indicative of the special relationship they shared. He never felt the need to sacrifice a young goat because everything that belonged to him belonged to his son, and they were always together.

WORDS FROM WESLEY

Luke 15:31

Thou art ever with me, and all that I have is thine—This suggests a strong reason against murmuring at the indulgence shown to the greatest of sinners. As the father's receiving the younger son did not cause him to disinherit the elder, so God's receiving notorious sinners will be no loss to those who have always served Him: neither will He raise these to a state of glory, equal to that of those who have always served Him, if they have, upon the whole, made a greater progress in inward as well as outward holiness. (ENNT)

The father insisted that the celebration was warranted because **this brother of yours was dead and is alive again; he was lost and is found** (v. 32). It is no small thing to go from death to life. Thus, rejoicing is the natural response to the new life that comes to those who are saved. When sinners are saved, their new status is worth celebrating. The gift of salvation does not come by trying, but rather by trusting.

What good news for sinners that our heavenly Father longs to embrace us! Though we are undeserving of God's grace, He lavishes it upon us anyway. We cannot earn our salvation. It is a free gift. Whenever someone receives this gift, like our Father, joy should flow from our souls. And we should find joy daily in serving God. What a privilege to be counted as a child of God! When was the last time you gave thanks for the unmerited favor of God in your life? Does your attitude resemble that of the Pharisees and teachers of the law in any way? Do you share the same passion for seeking the lost as your Father? Praise God today for His amazing grace.

DISCUSSION

Have you ever found something of considerable value? Perhaps you found lost car keys, a twenty-dollar bill, a dog, or a credit card. Finding that lost item made your day, didn't it? Jesus told three stories about "valuables" that were lost and then found.

1. In the parable of the loving father, do you think the runaway son represents an unbeliever or a wayward believer? Defend your answer.

2. Why do you think so many teenagers today run away from home?

3. What troubles do you believe runaway kids are most likely to encounter?

4. How might a church support parents of runaway kids?

5. Have you known someone who returned to God after reaching a low point in his or her life? What persuaded him or her to return to God?

6. Read Luke 15:25–30. How did the older brother's attitude reflect the attitude of the Pharisees?

7. How might a believer use Ecclesiastes 12:1 in counseling a Christian teenager who thinks worldly living is attractive?

8. How does the runaway son's father picture our heavenly Father?

PRAYER

Our Father in heaven, we have a fresh understanding of the lengths You went to in order to rescue us. We are grateful to know how much You love us. Help us serve You with love and appreciation in return.

YOU CAN CHANGE

Luke 18:18–30; 19:1–10

Life change is possible with God's help.

A Christian wrote a letter of apology to his former employer and enclosed a check to cover the cost of items he had pilfered when he was an employee. He explained in the letter that he had become a Christian after leaving the company and believed God wanted him to make as many things right as possible. He said he wanted his conscience to be clear.

When Zacchaeus welcomed Jesus into his life, he wanted to make restitution. He volunteered to give half his possessions to the poor, and, if he had cheated anyone, he said he would pay back four times the amount.

This study shows how God can change lives.

COMMENTARY

From chapter 15 through the middle of chapter 18, Luke recorded various teachings of Jesus, mostly in parables, as He traveled the road to Jericho. The last parable in this section illustrates Jesus' astonishing claim that the repentant sinner—a despised tax collector—would be "justified before God" (18:14) ahead of the self-righteous person—a Pharisee. Luke next recorded Jesus' calling children to himself and asserting that "anyone who will not receive the kingdom of God like a little child will never enter it" (v. 17)—to Jesus' hearers, another astonishing claim. This sets up the encounter with the young ruler, whom everyone assumed Jesus would commend as righteous because he was rich.

Immediately following the episode of the young ruler, Jesus once more predicted His death; then, as they approached Jericho, He healed a blind beggar. The encounter with Zacchaeus followed. This whole section of Luke set most people's expectations on their heads. Those everyone thought to be close to God, weren't; those they thought had no chance of salvation, did.

Jesus and the Rich Young Ruler (Luke 18:18–23)

All three Synoptic Gospels contain this story. Only Luke identified the man as a **ruler** (v. 18); only Matthew noted that he was "young" (Matt. 19:20, 22); only Mark recorded that Jesus "loved him" (Mark 10:21). From the three accounts together, we arrive at our usual designation of him as "the rich young ruler."

Jesus called out the young man on his form of address before addressing his question (Luke 18:19). Some writers take Jesus' comment as a denial that He himself was and is God. In light of the many occasions when Jesus did claim to be divine, it is better to hear in His response a gentle invitation for the young man to consider Jesus' divinity.

WORDS FROM WESLEY
Luke 18:22

Yet lackest thou one thing—Namely, to love God more than mammon. Our Saviour knew his heart, and presently put him upon a trial which laid it open to the ruler himself. And to cure his love of the world, which could not in him be cured otherwise, Christ commanded him to sell all that he had. But He does not command us to do this; but to use all to the glory of God. (ENNT)

By the usual Protestant numbering of the Ten Commandments, Jesus quoted numbers five through nine, in this order: seven, six, eight, nine, five. (Matthew and Mark have a slightly different order.) The young man responded promptly that he had **kept** them **since** he **was a boy** (v. 21). Jesus did not challenge him on this; outwardly, at least, it is possible for humans not to violate these standards, though Jesus' teaching in the Sermon on the Mount takes them to a deeper level (Matt. 5:17–48).

To this young man, Jesus did not say, "Be willing to sell," but **"Sell everything you have and give to the poor"** (Luke 18:22). Certainly as many have preached from this passage, Jesus calls on all His followers to be willing to give everything to follow Him. But this young man was asked to sell everything and give away the proceeds. We follow the spirit of Jesus' standard of discipleship here if we ask, not, "Am I willing to sell everything I have and give it away to follow Jesus?" but, "Do I acknowledge that everything I 'own' belongs to God already, to be disposed of as God directs?"

He became very sad (v. 23); Matthew and Mark add that he "went away sad" because he was not willing to part with his **great wealth**. This would mean **Jesus looked at him** (v. 24) as the young man walked away from Him, perhaps forever. Mark even noted that Jesus "loved him" (Mark 10:21). Jesus was sad, too, but for a different reason.

WORDS FROM WESLEY
Luke 18:23

The means to heal a sin-sick soul, to cure a foolish desire, an inordinate affection, are often painful, not in the nature of the thing, but from the nature of the disease. So when our Lord said to the rich young man, "Go, sell that thou hast, and give to the poor" (as well knowing, this was the only means of healing his covetousness), the very thought of it gave him so much pain, that "he went away sorrowful"; choosing rather to part with his hope of heaven, than his possessions on earth. This was a burden he could not consent to lift, a cross he would not take up. And in the one kind or the other, every follower of Christ. (WJW, vol. 6, 109)

Jesus and the Bystanders (Luke 18:24–30)

Jesus' statement, **"How hard it is for the rich to enter the kingdom of God!"** (v. 24), might not strike us as forcefully as it should. First, most of us have heard it often; it has become too familiar to us. Second, though we, too, may defer (unbiblically) to the rich, our theology does not let us say wealth is a sign of righteousness, as many of Jesus' hearers believed. Jesus' declaration was a flat-out contradiction of that common theology; it hit His first hearers hard.

It is easy to find the explanation that **the eye of a needle** (v. 25) was an informal name for a small gate in the wall of Jerusalem, through which a camel could not enter without first being stripped of its load and then kneeling. As attractive and enduring as this explanation has proven itself, it simply is not true. No such gate existed in ancient Jerusalem. Camels do not move when they are kneeling. The gates of Jerusalem probably did not have wickets, small gates set into or beside them, to avoid the necessity of opening the larger gate to admit only one or a few persons. Even if they did, they would not have admitted a camel, even without a load. Rather, Jesus' pronouncement is an example of the literary device of hyperbole, exaggeration for effect, to get a point across. Of course, a real camel cannot get through the tiny eye of a real sewing needle. Just so, the rich cannot enter the kingdom of God just because they are wealthy.

No wonder Jesus' hearers "were astonished," as both Matthew and Mark reported. Their question reflects their astonishment: **"Who then *can* be saved?"** (v. 26, emphasis added). Their popular theology said, "Their wealth proves the wealthy are saved." Jesus said, "The rich cannot be saved." If not the rich, then who?

But Jesus was not quite finished. He continued, saying, **"What is impossible with men is possible with God"** (v. 27). For the rich, who almost always trust their wealth—and their class or family or self-achievement, which secured it for them—salvation is more difficult than a camel's passing through the eye of a needle. The rich young ruler had just demonstrated that. But the rich need not despair; God's grace is extended even to them. They need, as do we all, only to respond with grateful acceptance.

Peter, speaking for the disciples as he often did, showed he had learned at least a part of the lesson (v. 28). The implied question behind Peter's bold assertion was "So, what's in it for us?"

Jesus' reply was both reassuring and much more gracious than Peter's bluntness. It consisted of a twofold promise. First, all are called to put Jesus first. Sometimes, circumstances then dictate that a person literally loses home, possessions, even all or part of one's family **for the sake of the kingdom of God** (v. 29).

If that happens, Jesus promised, His disciples will **receive many times as much in this age** (v. 30). Families who reject the believer are replaced by many more brothers and sisters in Christ. Families separated because of persecution, or because of some following the call to minister far away, will be reunited here or hereafter. In the meantime, many more brothers and sisters in Christ will become well-known and loved.

The second part of Jesus' promise reaches even further. **In the age to come** the one who has left all for Jesus, or has left all at Jesus' feet, will receive **eternal life** (v. 30). As usual, Peter (and we) received a God-sized answer to a child-sized question.

Jesus and the Short Sinner (Luke 19:1–10)

New Testament **Jericho** (v. 1) was a large and wealthy city. It had been the winter residence of the Hasmonean (Maccabean) dynasty. As their not-quite-legitimate heir, Herod the Great took it over and, as he did at many places, greatly expanded it. Jesus was coming south from Galilee; at Jericho, He turned right onto the Jerusalem road, upward and westward through the desolate Judean wilderness, close to where He had been tempted after His forty days of fasting.

The name **Zacchaeus** (v. 2) means innocent or pure. His station as a **chief tax collector** would have made his name a bitter irony to his Jewish countrymen, who had to pay him Rome's hated taxes. Most readers assume Zacchaeus's wealth came from extorting higher tax payments than Rome required, and pocketing the difference. This is possible, but not provable, given the complexities of taxation in Roman Judea; Zacchaeus may have been "innocent" of tax collection fraud.

WORDS FROM WESLEY
Luke 19:2

And he was rich—These words seem to refer to the discourse in the last chapter, ver. 24–27, particularly to ver. 27. Zacchaeus is a proof, that it is possible by the power of God, for even *a rich man to enter into the kingdom of heaven.* (ENNT)

When tourism still was a viable industry in Jericho, a few tour guides used to show tourists and pilgrims the very **sycamore-fig tree** Zacchaeus climbed to see Jesus (v. 4). Of course, it wasn't the same tree, but it was a sycamore (different from the North American sycamore). Even a short man can climb a sycamore easily because its sturdy branches begin to grow from the trunk only a few feet from the ground; perched on the second or third branch, Zacchaeus would have had a great vantage point to see Jesus, while shielded by the tree's leaves from the easy notice of the passersby.

Most people don't look up as they walk, especially if they are occupied with something on the ground, as the crowd was with Jesus. But reaching the tree where Zacchaeus was perched, Jesus looked directly at Zacchaeus. This was more than Zacchaeus had bargained for when he climbed the tree.

Furthermore, Jesus invited himself to Zacchaeus's house; the Greek clause is "For today in your house it is necessary for me to stay" (v. 5, paraphrase). Jesus intended to stay the night in Jericho, and Zacchaeus would be His host. Why it was necessary for Jesus to be his guest Zacchaeus would discover that very evening.

WORDS FROM WESLEY

Luke 19:5

Sinner, come down at Jesus' call,
Sink into thy own nothingness,
Feel the full misery of thy fall,
Thy vile apostasy confess,
Jesus with lowly faith receive,
Who stoops with sinful men to live.
Humility prepares His way.
His saving power the humble feel:
Jesus will lodge with thee to-day,
Will every day with sinners dwell,
But be their everlasting Feast.
He for no invitation stays,
But freely of His own accord
Comes with the kingdom of His grace,
And favour shows as sovereign Lord:
His love, for every sinner free,
Precedes all good desire in thee. (PW, vol. 11, 263–264)

Zacchaeus's response to Jesus' words was, literally, rejoicing (v. 6). The crowd's response was opposite: **All the people saw this and began to mutter "He has gone to be the guest of a 'sinner'"** (v. 7). Again, the crucial point, in their minds, was up front for emphasis: "With a sinful man." Given the past tense of the main verb, and what follows in verses 8–10, we may assume the crowd's grumbling began as Zacchaeus descended the tree, and continued as he, Jesus, and others reclined for the feast.

Zacchaeus knew where he stood with the people of Jericho; he also knew his own heart and what Jesus was doing for him by coming to his house. So he **stood up** from his couch at his own feast (v. 8); the short sinner stood tall in generosity and repentance. We should not overlook that Zacchaeus also called Jesus **Lord**.

There is reason to think Zacchaeus's cheating of taxpayers was less than usually assumed; it is possible he had cheated no one. He hardly could have paid fourfold restitution to those he had cheated and have given half his goods to the poor if most of his wealth had come from extortionate tax collections. The offer of fourfold restitution fits the Pentateuchal requirement for making good on stolen livestock (Ex. 22:1).

Jesus acknowledged Zacchaeus's repentance, saying, **"Today salvation has come to this house"** (Luke 19:9). **Salvation** is from the same Greek root as in the bystanders' question of 18:26: "Who then can be saved?" Zacchaeus, too, was a rich man, but unlike the rich young ruler, he stopped trusting in his wealth when he met Jesus.

This may be an indirect assertion of Jesus' divine status by Luke the gospel writer (who offered direct assertions, as well). If salvation for the rich (as, of course, for all of us) is possible only with God, and if Zacchaeus, a rich man, found salvation upon meeting Jesus, the implication, at least, is that Jesus is God.

Zacchaeus was **a son of Abraham** (19:9) by nationality, of course; he was Jewish, as his name, the Greek form of Hebrew *Zaccai*, demonstrates. More importantly, he now also was a son of Abraham by faith, as Paul later would explain so eloquently (Gal. 3:6–9, 26–29).

All those who observed Jesus' interaction with these two men assumed the rich young ruler was saved; his wealth demonstrated that, according to their theological understanding. All also assumed Zacchaeus was lost because his wealth came from collecting

Rome's taxes; indeed, he affirmed their assumption by his repentance. But the young ruler turned from Jesus and, thus, from salvation, while Zacchaeus found salvation by turning from his wealth to Jesus. Indeed, said Jesus in conclusion, that was why He had come: **to seek and to save what was lost** (Luke 19:10). Many have believed Jesus told the truth in this "mission statement." Like Zacchaeus, they have found salvation in Him.

DISCUSSION

Although it is not wrong to own numerous possessions, it is wrong to let possessions own us. A man who had not only riches, but also authority over others, valued wealth above Jesus.

1. Read Luke 18:18. Do you think there is a clue in this verse that suggests how the ruler became rich? If so, what is it?

2. Why do you agree or disagree that prosperity is a sign of godliness?

3. Read 1 Timothy 6:6–10. How should a believer relate to material possessions?

4. Why do you agree or disagree that money is the root of all evil?

5. Read Luke 19:1–10. Why do you think Zacchaeus was so interested in seeing Jesus?

6. What does it say about Jesus that He wanted to stay at Zacchaeus's house?

7. Read Luke 19:7. Why should we not allow negative criticism to influence our evangelistic efforts?

8. What evidence of genuine conversion did Zacchaeus provide?

9. How would you answer someone who claims that Jesus came to earth to found a religion or become a martyr?

PRAYER

Lord Jesus, like Zacchaeus, we choose to seek and follow You. We want to please You in all ways, especially in handling the resources You've entrusted to us. Show us what to do, and help us obey Your direction.

12

AFTER FAILURE

Luke 22:1–6, 20–23, 31–32, 54–62

The way we respond to failure has consequences for us and for others.

We are never immune to failure, and if we fail to rely on the Lord in every situation, the failure will occur quickly and dramatically. Joshua failed to capture the little town of Ai due to self-confidence. David diverted his attention from the Lord and onto Bathsheba. We know how his failure wrecked his family, ripped his soul, and shamed the nation. After winning a great victory over the prophets of Baal, Elijah ran for his life when Jezebel threatened him. Deep in the desert he held a private pity party. But God restored each of those men to fellowship and victory.

This study reminds us that God is the God of second chances.

COMMENTARY

Between Jesus' triumphal entry into Jerusalem on the Sunday before the Passover (Luke 19:28–46) and the beginning of our study here, Luke records a number of Jesus' teachings and representative encounters during the first half of Holy Week. Luke 22 opens with Judas's arrangement to betray Jesus. Our study verses end with Peter's denials following Jesus' arrest. In Luke's narrative, Jesus' trials before the various authorities follow, then the crucifixion, death, burial, and resurrection.

Our first focus is on Judas's betrayal and Peter's denial of Jesus. Both were serious offenses against the friend both had followed for three years. Peter's offense was, in its way, no less serious than Judas's, and we shall not minimize it. But the contrast between the responses of the two when they realized what they had done is even more instructive. Judas regretted his betrayal, but did not follow his regret with repentance. Peter repented and experienced both the humiliation and joy of restoration. Indeed, failure does not have to be final.

Judas's Plot to Betray Jesus (Luke 22:1–6)

The name **Feast of Unleavened Bread** (v. 1) comes from Moses' instruction to Israel not to leaven their bread on the eve of the exodus from Egypt (Ex. 12:8, 14). The name **Passover** (Luke 22:1) recalls the death angel's "passing over" Israelite homes, while killing the Egyptian firstborn (Ex. 12:12–13, 29–30). At the inception of Jesus' public ministry, His cousin John had declared Him God's Passover Lamb (John 1:29).

The chief priests (Luke 22:2) were, for the most part, of the Sadducean party, which controlled the priesthood during this period. Most **teachers of the law**, or scribes, were Pharisees or allied with them. Since the Pharisees and Sadducees were on opposite sides in most controversies, Luke's report emphasizes both parties' hatred of Jesus in their cooperation to find a **way to get rid of** Him (v. 2). As the English phrase usually does today, the Greek verb here denotes their intention to kill Jesus.

Jesus' triumphal entry (Luke 19:28–46) had underscored His popularity with the people, and His teaching in and near the temple in the following days had only increased it, for most of His hearers recognized Jesus' integrity and the truth of His teachings. The leadership had good reason to fear the people should they try to arrest Him or even to stop Him from teaching. Practically speaking, they needed to arrest Jesus at night.

The fact that **Satan entered Judas** (22:3) does not mean Judas had no choice. Even Jesus' statement in His High Priestly Prayer about "the one doomed to destruction so that Scripture would be fulfilled" (John 17:12) does not mean Judas was without choice. True, the prediction of Jesus' betrayal (Ps. 41:9) would be fulfilled, but Judas could have chosen not to be the one to fulfill it.

WORDS FROM WESLEY

Luke 22:3

Then entered Satan—Who is never wanting to assist those [who never avoids assisting those], whose heart is bent upon mischief. (ENNT)

Many have speculated on Judas's motivation for betraying Jesus and his initiating the discussion with **the chief priests and the officers of the temple guard** (Luke 22:4). Judas's remorse when he saw that Jesus really was condemned to crucifixion (Matt. 27:1–10) probably rules out hatred of Jesus as his motivation. He simply may have been greedy, unable to resist this chance for substantial personal gain.

Given that greed is but the least complex form of the lust to power, it seems perhaps more likely that Judas hoped to force Jesus' hand. By getting Him arrested, Judas hoped to make Jesus use His power to save himself when push came to shove; he then would share in Jesus' power and glory. If this was Judas's motive, it shows he did not believe Jesus' repeated statements about His real mission until it was too late.

An opportunity (Luke 22:6) is, literally, a good time or moment; there is irony here for the believer in Jesus. Judas's good time would have seemed, to the outsider, to have been Jesus' bad time. Yet, in the fulfillment of God's cosmic purposes, Jesus turned Judas's and Satan's good time into the worst moment of all for them, and the moment of His own eternal triumph over sin and death.

Jesus' Prediction of Judas's Betrayal (Luke 22:20–23)

The intervening verses are a brief record of Jesus' last Passover with the Twelve, called in Christian tradition the Last Supper. **After the supper he took the cup** (v. 20); this probably was the fourth and last cup in the traditional Passover meal. As the poured-out blood of the Passover lamb had foreshadowed the ultimate Passover Lamb, now that Lamb, Jesus, used the fourth cup, the "blood of the grape," as a symbol of His **blood, which is poured out for you** (v. 20; the Twelve, and all believers of every age).

WORDS FROM WESLEY
Luke 22:20

This is called *The New Testament in Christ's blood*, which could not possibly mean, that it was the New Testament itself, but only the seal of it, and the sign of that blood which was shed to confirm it. (ENNT)

Jesus knew what was about to happen and who intended to betray Him. We may take Jesus' prediction of Judas's act and His warning to him as a final effort to dissuade and save Judas, not himself. Yes, the fact of Jesus' betrayal had been predicted long ago, even **decreed** (v. 22), but even at that late hour, Judas still retained his choice to renounce the course he had agreed on with the temple authorities.

Before the fact, it is obvious none of the disciples suspected Judas would be the betrayer (v. 23). John reported that even after Jesus had identified Judas, some of the Twelve thought, when Judas left the meal, that he went on an errand for Jesus, not against Him (John 13:29). Luke's less-specific account on this detail leaves room for the reader to reflect on the fact that any or all of us could betray Jesus if we do not consistently lean on His strength rather than our own.

Jesus' Reassuring Words to Simon Peter (Luke 22:31–32)

From doubting themselves or perhaps each other, the Eleven (Luke does not mention Judas's departure) turned to arguing about which of them was greatest (v. 24). Jesus' response was another attempt to help them see what kingdom greatness is.

At the end of this short "lecture," Jesus addressed Simon Peter, whom we are prone to name as the greatest of the Eleven. The reader knows already that "Satan [had] entered Judas" (v. 3). Jesus' announcement, that **Satan** had **asked** for **Simon** also (v. 31), prompts the mental protest, "No, not another of the inner circle!" The word translated **has asked** denotes an intensive, persistent, careful inquiry; Satan really wanted Peter, as he had obtained Judas.

Jesus reassured Simon that He had **prayed for** him, **that** his **faith** would **not fail** (v. 32). This raises the question, "Did Jesus pray for Judas, too?" Undoubtedly, He did; Jesus prayed for all His followers regularly. But Judas already had chosen another path and had left. Judas was not present to hear Jesus tell him He had prayed for him in this hour of strong temptation.

WORDS FROM WESLEY
Luke 22:32

But I have prayed for thee—Who wilt be in the greatest danger of all: *that thy faith fail not*—Altogether: *And when thou art returned*—From thy flight, *strengthen thy brethren*—All that are weak in faith; perhaps scandalized at thy fall. (ENNT)

As we will see in the next section, Peter's faith did fail temporarily, so to speak. But at a deeper level, Peter's faith did not fail; when Jesus merely looked at him after his third denial, Peter went out bitterly remorseful and eventually was restored. This restoration Jesus foreshadowed in His instruction, **when you have turned back**—when you have repented of your coming lapse in loyalty to Him—**strengthen your brothers** (v. 32).

Peter's Denial of Jesus (Luke 22:54–62)

Jesus led the Eleven from the upper room within the city of Jerusalem, eastward across the Kidron Valley to the garden of Gethsemane on a lower slope of the Mount of Olives. There He prayed; there Judas found Him, as he expected, and had Jesus arrested.

Peter and John (John 18:15–16), at least, **followed at a distance** back into the city, **into the house of the high priest** (Luke 22:54). Caiaphas was high priest at this time, though his father-in-law, Annas, still held the real priestly power. Tradition and archaeological investigation place Caiaphas' house just outside the present southern wall of Jerusalem's Old City, under the Church of St. Peter in Gallicantu ("St. Peter of the cockcrowing").

This Passover probably occurred in early April, which can have chilly evenings in Jerusalem, one-half mile above sea level. **A fire in the middle of the courtyard** (v. 55) was an excellent idea.

Peter had been the one to strike a blow in Jesus' defense in the garden, before Jesus told him to put his sword away (John 18:10–11). He had followed Jesus into the high priest's own courtyard. Now he made so bold as to slip in and sit down near the fire among the temple guards and servants of the high priest's household. We need not fault Peter for lack of courage, normally.

All the more ironic, then, that the statement of a "mere" **servant girl** (Luke 22:56) unnerved Peter. She certainly had not been present at Jesus' arrest in the garden. She either had seen Peter with Jesus on another occasion or guessed his association with Jesus from his entrance into the courtyard with John (John 18:16). This first denial (Luke 22:57) did not trigger in Peter any memory of Jesus' prediction only a few hours earlier. The second person to assert Peter's association with Jesus was a man. Peter's second denial was a bit stronger. He said, **"Man, I am not!"** (v. 58). His reply indicated Peter's increasing frustration, irritation, and fear. The third person to confront Peter did so on the basis of his being **a Galilean** (v. 59). Denial of that would have been pointless; Peter's speech (dialect and/or accent) and perhaps his clothes gave him away. Instead, he replied with an even stronger denial of knowing Jesus (v. 60). Both Matthew and Mark reported that with his third denial, Peter uttered a curse against himself should he be lying (Matt. 26:74; Mark 14:71).

WORDS FROM WESLEY

Luke 22:59

And about one hour after—So he did not recollect himself in all that time. (ENNT)

Peter's three denials had not been enough to remind him of Jesus' prediction. But he hardly had finished his third denial when **the rooster crowed** (Luke 22:60). At the same time, **the Lord turned and looked straight at Peter** (v. 61). These two events together, sound and sight—from the rooster, lord of the dawn, and from Jesus, whom he had declared Lord of his life— broke Peter. **He went outside and wept bitterly** (v. 62).

Both Judas and Peter regretted failing Jesus. Judas's regret, however, did not lead to repentance, while Peter's regret did. Filled with remorse, Peter pondered Jesus' assurance of His prayers for him (vv. 31–32).

Peter was present twice when Jesus showed himself to the disciples in Jerusalem, but it was not until the breakfast on the shore of Galilee that Jesus assured Peter he was forgiven and restored

(John 21:15–19). Perhaps the smaller group was necessary; on this occasion only seven of the Eleven were present (John 21:2). Perhaps Peter needed time; sometimes it is easier to accept others' forgiveness than to forgive ourselves.

The gospel writers seem at least to imply that even Judas would have been forgiven had he repented rather than committed suicide. Peter did repent and became a vigorous witness to Jesus' life, death, and resurrection, even in his own death years later in Rome. Peter's example should give us hope when we fail, and encourage us to extend God's grace to others when they fail. Failure does not have to be final.

DISCUSSION

Life holds many disappointments, but perhaps none are bigger than those we encounter when friends let us down or betray us. Jesus experienced denial and betrayal by so-called friends.

1. Read Luke 22:1 and Exodus 12:3–7. How did Jesus, the Lamb of God, fulfill the requirements involved in each Hebrew family's selection of a lamb in Egypt?

2. Read Luke 22:2. Why do you agree or disagree that certain religious and/or political leaders today would like to "get rid of Jesus"?

3. Why did the chief priests and officers of the temple want to take custody of Jesus when no crowd was present?

4. Why do you agree or disagree that it is possible today to betray Jesus for money?

5. How was Satan involved in previous schemes to get rid of Jesus?

6. Read Luke 22:54–63. Do you believe it is possible today to follow Jesus "at a distance" (v. 54)? Why or why not?

7. Compare Luke 22:56–60 and John 21:15–17. What connection, if any, do you see between the three denials and the three questions about Peter's love for Jesus?

8. What situations today might test a believer's loyalty to Jesus?

9. How do you know the Lord completely forgave and restored Peter?

PRAYER

God, as we look back, we feel great remorse for the times we've failed You. More than that, we feel a burning desire to be restored and to withstand temptation next time. Grant us Your strength to stand strong for You.

RESOURCES FOR THE TOUGH TIMES

Luke 23:1–7, 13–25

When faced with intolerance, intimidation, and injustice, the child
of God has great spiritual resources available.

Contrary to what some people believe, Jesus did not die because
He was weak. He was strong. He did not die as a martyr. He died
as our Savior. No one took His life. He freely gave it up for us.
Calvary was not a disaster. It was a triumph. The crucifixion was
not carried out simply by the will of an angry mob. It was carried
out by Jesus to fulfill the Father's will. Nails did not keep Jesus
on the cross. His love for the entire world and us kept Him there.

This study helps us understand why Jesus died, and it instills
in us a greater love for Him.

COMMENTARY

The temple authorities had found Jesus guilty of blasphemy,
though whether they conducted a formal trial has been the subject
of considerable debate. Blasphemy was a capital offense, according
to the Pentateuchal Law. On the basis of Jesus' accusers' statement
found in John 18:31, it is often asserted that the right to impose
the death sentence was reserved to the Roman governor, but that,
too, is debated. Whether of necessity or because they wished to avoid
direct responsibility for His death, the temple leadership brought
Jesus to Pilate.

Pilate was prefect of Judea from A.D. 26 to 36. His usual residence
was in Caesarea Maritima, the capital of the province, but he
came to Jerusalem before the Passover to be on hand with extra
troops in the hope of preventing disturbances. Pilate provoked

his Jewish subjects several times during his tenure; he may have given in to the demand for Jesus' crucifixion because he felt he could not afford another complaint to Caesar. Pilate finally was removed for using unnecessary and excessive force against the Samaritans.

In this study, note the contrast between Pilate and Jesus. Jesus possessed all power but chose not to use it to save himself. Pilate's power was delegated from Caesar in Rome, but he could not bring himself to do the right thing and release Jesus, because he feared the people Caesar had sent him to rule. Character is revealed in crisis.

Pilate's First Encounter with Jesus (Luke 23:1–7)

Most of the ruling council, the Sanhedrin, had concluded Jesus was guilty of blasphemy. Only one or two, apparently, thought He could be telling the truth. That **the whole assembly rose and led him off to Pilate** (v. 1) is an indication of their intense interest in Jesus' case and the animosity most felt toward Him. The more usual approach would have been to send Him under guard with two or three council members to present the charges against Him.

This time, almost everyone wanted to be part of the action. The first charge, **He opposes payment of taxes to Caesar** (v. 2), was false. When asked that very question, Jesus had said to give to Caesar what belonged to Caesar (Luke 20:20–26).

WORDS FROM WESLEY
Luke 23:4

Then said Pilate—After having heard His defence—*I find no fault in this man*—I do not find that He either asserts or attempts any thing seditious or injurious to Cesar. (ENNT)

The second charge Pilate sought to verify by Jesus' own testimony. When he asked Him directly whether He was **the king of the Jews** (23:3), Jesus' answer was, "You say," usually translated similarly to the NIV's **"Yes, it is as you say"** (v. 3).

Why, then, did Pilate announce, **"I find no basis for a charge against this man"** (v. 4)? Luke gives no hint, but John's account records at least part of a conversation between Jesus and Pilate, in which Jesus affirmed His kingship, but in terms clearly representing no political threat to Caesar (John 18:34–37; 19:11). Jesus' strange words caused Pilate to maneuver desperately to avoid responsibility for condemning Him.

WORDS FROM WESLEY

Luke 23:4

Harmless in act, and word, and thought,
The judge declares Him free from blame,
Without a blemish or a spot,
A sinless Saint, a perfect Lamb;
And such is a fit sacrifice,
And such for sinful man He dies! (PW, vol. 11, 296–297)

The temple authorities tried again, but their next phrasing of their charges gave Pilate an opening. **He stirs up the people** (Luke 23:5) is vague, as criminal charges go. They intended to give Pilate the impression that Jesus had a specifically political, or even military, agenda, as many self-styled messiahs actually did in first-century Judea and Galilee. But when Jesus' accusers mentioned Galilee, trying to leave the impression that Jesus was finding success in spreading His insurrection from a region quite far away from Judea, Pilate's direct and personal responsibility, Pilate seized on the opportunity and sent Jesus to Herod (vv. 6–7).

Herod Antipas, a son of Herod the Great, was tetrarch of Galilee—north of Judea and separated from it by Samaria—and Perea, across the Jordan from Judea. Thus, Herod was the ruler (under Caesar) of whom Jesus was the earthly political subject. If Jesus was accused of starting His insurrection in Galilee, Pilate was only too happy to send Him across town and let Herod deal with Him.

While in Jerusalem, Pilate stayed in the western palace built by Herod the Great. This palace was located in what is now the Armenian (southwestern) Quarter of the Old City. It was much grander and more comfortable than the Antonia Fortress adjacent to the temple (also built/rebuilt by Herod the Great) and befit Pilate's station as the ranking Roman administrator. (This new understanding is derived from archaeological investigations in Jerusalem over the past four decades; it requires a small adjustment from the traditional locations of some stops between Jesus' Gethsemane arrest and the crucifixion.)

Herod Antipas's Jerusalem residence most likely was the Hasmonean palace just west of the temple complex, a little more than a quarter mile east of the western palace where Pilate stayed. (The Herods were Hasmonean heirs, also.)

Herod was in Jerusalem for the Passover because the Herodians wished their Jewish subjects to think they were devoted to the worship of God. Antipas's devotion left much to be desired, however, as we learn from his personal life and from his execution of John the Baptist. His shallowness is shown in his delight at the chance to interrogate Jesus, but only in the hope that he might persuade Jesus to perform a miracle for him (v. 8). Failing in that endeavor, failing to elicit even a word from Jesus, Herod mocked Jesus by draping Him in the "royal" purple and sending Him back to Pilate.

Pilate's Second Attempt to Release Jesus (Luke 23:13–17)

Pilate still hoped to avoid responsibility for Jesus. To this end, he reviewed for the crowd the steps he had taken as the scrupulous, honest judge: (1) he carefully repeated their charge against Jesus: **"You bought** Him **as one who was inciting the people to rebellion"**; (2) he reminded them, **"I have examined him in your presence"**—meaning they had seen he did nothing unjust; (3) he reminded them, **"I . . . have found no basis for your charges against him"** (v. 14). They had found Pilate harsh and unjust in the past; perhaps his vigorous defense of a clearly innocent Jewish man would earn him points now.

Pilate had an additional point in his favor this time around, or so he thought. Herod now had examined Jesus, also, and had **sent him back** (v. 15). Herod Antipas was the son of a paranoid father who had killed several of his own sons, and his favorite wife, because he suspected they had designs on his kingdom. Antipas had survived intrigues and insurrections himself, in his thirty years as tetrarch. If Antipas detected no political threat, Jesus was no political threat.

"I will punish him" (v. 16); the Greek word means, basically, "instruct, discipline." From the negative aspects of discipline, it acquired the sense of **punish**, Pilate's meaning here. In practice, such official "discipline" was administered with whips. Pilate offered to have Jesus scourged, though He had **done nothing . . . then release him** (vv. 15–16).

Verse 17 is lacking in most of the better Greek manuscripts. English versions now place it as a footnote (for example, NIV) or within brackets (for example, NASB). The NIV reads, **Now he was obliged to release one man to them at the Feast.** This explanatory note does occur in Matthew 27:15; Mark 15:6; and John 18:39. Apparently a later copyist decided it belongs in Luke, also; perhaps he thought an earlier copyist had deleted it by mistake. We should note that instead of **he was obliged**, the other gospel writers recorded that it was "customary"; that difference is another reason to think this notice is not original in Luke.

Pilate's Capitulation (Luke 23:18–25)

If verse 17 does not belong in Luke, still Luke took it for granted that his readers would know of the custom, for he continued his narrative with the response of the crowd that they wanted Jesus condemned and **Barabbas** (v. 18) released.

WORDS FROM WESLEY
Luke 23:20

O what mercy hath God prepared for you, if you do not trample it under foot! "What mercy hath He prepared for them that fear Him, even before the sons of men!" A peace which the world cannot give; joy, that no man taketh from you; rest from doubt and fear and sorrow of heart; and love, the beginning of heaven. And are not these for you? Are they not all purchased for you by Him who loved you, and gave himself for you? For you, a sinner? You, a rebel against God? You, who have so long crucified Him afresh? Now "look unto Him whom you have pierced!" Now say, Lord, it is enough. I have fought against thee long enough. I yield, I yield. "Jesus, Master, have mercy upon me!" (WJW, vol. 11, 165–166)

Luke's detail that they cried out **with one voice** (v. 18) hints at manipulation of the crowd during this phase of Pilate's hearing. Surely, it did not occur to everyone independently and simultaneously to ask for Barabbas instead of Jesus. Those who wanted Jesus condemned from the beginning had been whispering this suggestion through the crowd in anticipation of just this moment. Either that, or a few of them shouted Barabbas's name, and the crowd took it up immediately.

The irony of the situation, laid out for the reader in Luke's explanation of verse 19, could not have escaped anyone at that time; certainly it did not escape Pilate. They had brought Jesus to him under a false charge of **insurrection** (v. 19). Now they were demanding the release of a bona fide insurrectionist who had committed murder (probably in the course of his insurrection), to secure the execution of the innocent man.

Luke's plain and simple narrative of verse 20 eloquently reveals Pilate's increasing desperation. We have no reason to doubt the sincerity of his desire to release Jesus. John's narrative reveals that Jesus had made a profound impression on Pilate. Furthermore, we have Matthew's witness of Pilate's wife's dream and her message to her husband: "Don't have anything to do with that innocent man" (Matt. 27:19). But the crowd was just as determined that Jesus not be released. For the first time, Luke used the word **crucify** (Luke 23:21); they cried, literally, **"Crucify him! Crucify him!"**

For the third time (v. 22); that is, the third time Pilate had addressed the crowd since Herod had sent Jesus back to him. This is the fourth time Pilate said emphatically, **"I have found in him no grounds for the death penalty"** (here, and v. 15) or, more generally, "for a charge against him" (23:4, 14).

WORDS FROM WESLEY
Luke 23:22

He said to them the third time, Why, what evil hath he done? — As Peter, a disciple of Christ, dishonoured Him by denying Him thrice, so Pilate, a heathen, honoured Christ by thrice owning Him to be innocent. (ENNT)

The image that should come to mind from Luke's language in verse 23 is of nearly everyone in the assembled crowd shouting, **"Crucify him!"** (v. 21) — shouting it over and over, louder and louder, with the intent of drowning out Pilate's voice, should he attempt to reason with them again. **Their shouts prevailed** (v. 23) has a dual meaning. Initially, this report means simply that their prolonged shouting engulfed every other sound and made impossible the suggestion of any other alternative. Ultimately, their prolonged shouting prevailed over Pilate's four-times-expressed better judgment, and he surrendered to **their demand** (v. 24).

Luke's spare depiction of this scene does not allow for the anti-Semitic fastening of the guilt for Jesus' death upon all the Jewish people for all time. Still, it may be a helpful reminder, even when considering Luke's narrative, that to read Matthew's and John's accounts that way is to misread them also. It is dishonest to blame all Jews for Jesus' death, even only all the Jews of that generation, or only all the Jews of Jerusalem then. It is a paradoxical fact of God's grace that every human being shares equal responsibility for Jesus' death.

The power and pathos of Luke's account lies in his straightforward, judicious understatement, and in his juxtaposition of the appositive **the one they asked for** with **surrendered Jesus** (v. 25), placed first in the final clause for emphasis. Luke invited the reader to pause, ponder, and picture what we well know ensued from Pilate's abject surrender to the crowd.

Going in, Pilate thought he held all the power in this situation—both over Jesus and the accusing crowd. But with the moment of decision, Pilate's true character showed through; he neither stood up for Jesus nor to the crowd before him.

The only Hero in this scene is Jesus, whose character shone brightly. Truly possessing all power, He declined to use it for His own transitory good, laying it down, instead, for a nobler, eternal purpose, "to bring multitudes to glory" along with himself.

DISCUSSION

Our justice system is not perfect, but it does promise a fair trial and consider each person on trial to be innocent until proven guilty. Jesus did not receive a fair trial, and He was sentenced to death although He was fully innocent.

1. How did Jesus relate to the civil government during His public ministry?

2. Why do you agree or disagree that Jesus practiced civil disobedience?

3. What three adjectives would you use to describe Herod?

4. Why is it significant that Jesus died on a cross that had been prepared for someone else?

5. How do you explain the contrast between the jubilant welcome Jesus received when He entered Jerusalem and the treatment He received from the crowd Pilate addressed?

6. Read Matthew 27:19. Do you think Pilate's wife had become a believer in Jesus? Why or why not?

7. Read John 10:11 and 18. Ultimately, who decided Jesus would be crucified?

8. Read Galatians 1:4. Why did Jesus die?

PRAYER

Dear Jesus, we see now that we could have been one of the crowd calling out for Your blood. Yet You went willingly to pay our ransom. No words could express our wonder and gratefulness for Your unspeakable sacrifice.

WORDS FROM WESLEY WORKS CITED

ENNT: *Explanatory Notes upon the New Testament,* by John Wesley, M.A. Fourth American Edition. New York: J. Soule and T. Mason, for the Methodist Episcopal Church in the United States, 1818.

JCW: Wesley, C. (1849). *The Journal of the Rev. Charles Wesley.* (T. Jackson, Ed.) (Vol. 1–2). London: John Mason.

PW: *The Poetical Works of John and Charles Wesley.* Edited by D. D. G. Osborn. 13 vols. London: Wesleyan-Methodist Conference Office, 1868.

SCW: Wesley, Charles. *Sermons by the Late Rev. Charles Wesley.* London: Baldwin, Cradock, and Joy, 1816.

WJW: *The Works of John Wesley.* Third Edition, Complete and Unabridged. 14 vols. London: Wesleyan Methodist Book Room, 1872.

OTHER BOOKS IN THE
WESLEY BIBLE STUDIES SERIES

Genesis (available February 2015)
Exodus (available April 2015)
Leviticus through Deuteronomy (available June 2015)
Joshua through Ruth (available June 2015)
1 Samuel through 2 Chronicles (available February 2015)
Ezra through Esther (available April 2015)
Job through Song of Songs (available February 2015)
Isaiah (available April 2015)
Jeremiah through Daniel (available February 2015)
Hosea through Malachi (available June 2015)
Matthew
Mark
Luke
John
Acts
Romans
1–2 Corinthians
Galatians through Colossians and Philemon
1–2 Thessalonians
1 Timothy through Titus
Hebrews
James
1–2 Peter and Jude
1–3 John
Revelation

Now Available in the Wesley Bible Studies Series

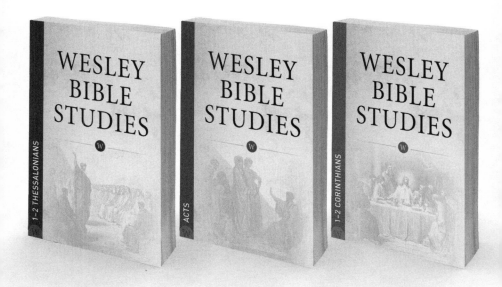

Each book in the Wesley Bible Studies series provides a thoughtful and powerful survey of key Scriptures in one or more biblical books. They combine accessible commentary from contemporary teachers, with relevantly highlighted direct quotes from the complete writings and life experiences of John Wesley, along with the poetry and hymns of his brother Charles. For each study, creative and engaging questions foster deeper fellowship and growth.

1–2 Thessalonians
978-0-89827-874-3
978-0-89827-875-0 (e-book)

Acts
978-0-89827-882-8
978-0-89827-883-5 (e-book)

1–2 Corinthians
978-0-89827-884-2
978-0-89827-885-9 (e-book)

wphonline.com
1.800.493.7539